Anna Theresa Sadlier

Pauline Archer

Anna Theresa Sadlier

Pauline Archer

ISBN/EAN: 9783741192630

Manufactured in Europe, USA, Canada, Australia, Japa

Cover: Foto ©Andreas Hilbeck / pixelio.de

Manufactured and distributed by brebook publishing software (www.brebook.com)

Anna Theresa Sadlier

Pauline Archer

PAULINE ARCHER.

BY

ANNA T. SADLIER.

New York, Cincinnati, Chicago:
BENZIGER BROTHERS,

COPYRIGHT, 1899, BY BENZIGER BROTHERS

Printed in the United States of America.

CONTENTS.

CHAPTER I.
PAULINE.. 7

CHAPTER II.
PAULINE'S FATHER............................. 16

CHAPTER III.
LITTLE MARY KELLY........................... 28

CHAPTER IV.
AN UNEXPECTED PLEASURE................ 40

CHAPTER V.
THE AFTERNOON AT THE PARK............ 46

CHAPTER VI.
THE SAME STORY DIFFERENTLY TOLD... 59

CHAPTER VII.
LITTLE MARY'S LAST VISIT................... 67

Contents.

CHAPTER VIII.
Why Little Mary Did Not Come 78

CHAPTER IX.
Pauline Goes Visiting 88

CHAPTER X.
Pauline's Cousins 98

CHAPTER XI.
A Luncheon at Aunt Lulu's 108

CHAPTER XII.
A Journey 116

CHAPTER XIII.
Rebecca Gets a Fright 126

CHAPTER XIV.
A New Playmate 137

CHAPTER XV.
A Delightful Excursion 143

CHAPTER XVI.
An Adventure and a Farewell 153

CHAPTER XVII.
Conclusion. Pauline at Home 163

PAULINE ARCHER.

CHAPTER I.

PAULINE.

PAULINE had been the daintiest of babies. When she had been taken out in her baby-carriage, the passers-by had noted her big blue eyes and yellow hair with lively admiration. In the second stage of her life's journey, when her uncertain little feet had trodden the pavement, she was still noticeable for a daintiness of form, feature, and dress, surrounding her like an atmosphere. From the very first she was upright in her carriage, while her blue eyes seemed to be looking onward and upward into some fairer country.

At the age of twelve she was still what the servants and other people of the same class who came in contact with her emphatically called " a little lady." Her parents had taken up their abode in a neighborhood which, without being precisely fashionable, was very genteel—one of those up-town streets of New York where there is a quietude in the midst of adjacent bustle, and where the noisy thoroughfares at either end in no wise disturb the peace which reigns in the middle of the block.

On sunny mornings one side of the street was in a blaze of glory, while the other was overshadowed by the great, dark, brown-stone houses. In the glory of this sunshine Pauline was often seen to walk, in the neatest of frocks, with spotless collar, or a frill at her throat and wrists, with carefully brushed shining hair, and hands white, with pink-tipped nails. Sometimes she carried a doll; but about the time when this story opens, when the long, hot summer was soon to give way to autumn and Pauline was about twelve years old, she began to have misgivings. Perhaps a great girl of her age should no longer carry a doll.

Still she was very, very loath to part with this cherished companion of babyhood, and her big blue eyes looked sadly down upon its somewhat faded garments and somewhat battered waxen face. She began to realize that the time for such things was nearly over and that she had almost reached the parting of the ways. A tear sometimes forced its way down her cheeks, falling upon her dainty frock, as she thought of the desolation in which the doll would some day be left, and how lonely she would then be.

She could not always confide her thoughts to any one, for Pauline's mother was an invalid whom she could see only at intervals, and her father was very busy. But she kept them in her own mind, some very curious little conceits, as she played about in the sunshine, sometimes skipping, sometimes running very fast, with a deer-like swiftness and lightness, and sometimes pacing up and down in her slow and thoughtful way.

She did not know much of the actual children of the neighborhood. Many of them went to school, so that she rarely saw them. But one of her greatest trials was the occasional incursion from some of the avenues, far west, of a horde of street-boys, who persecuted her with unwelcome attentions, saluting her with a variety of shouts:

"There goes Miss Proudie! Say, look at the big baby with her doll. Ain't she a daisy!"

The little girl never appeared to take any notice of these proceedings. She would not turn her head to look at her tormentors; and when she encountered them, as they hopped about in front of her mockingly, she only let her eyes rest upon them, not angrily nor haughtily, but only gravely and wonderingly. But it was their taunts that first made her hesitate about bringing out her beloved doll, to whom she used to apologize in her quaint way for having to leave it at home.

Once she confided her difficulties with these street arabs to her former nurse, Rebecca, who still in great measure had the care of her.

"And why don't you tell them to hold their saucy tongues?" asked that worthy woman indignantly.

"Oh, I wouldn't!" said Pauline, elevating her brows till they met, in her horror at the idea. "I never speak to any one in the street; I'm too much ashamed."

"Well, I guess if I go out to them I'll make some of them ashamed," said the nurse, retreating into her own room, with a sniff. She was usually occupied now in sewing, as her duties with regard to Pauline were very light. The existence of Rebecca became in some way known to Pauline's enemies, who saluted her with new taunts:

"Miss Proudie's got a nurse," they cried. "Oh, a big girl like that with a nurse!"

Pauline walked slowly up and down once or twice, as if to show that she was not so easily driven from the field, never looking towards the Eighth Avenue contingent, some of whom were astride the railing of a neighboring stoop. Then she passed slowly up, and sat down on the top step, near her own door, where the sunshine enfolded her as with a glory. She was feeling very lonely, for her little heart had failed her when she thought of taking out her doll. It would only expose her to new jeers.

The boys, tired of their sport, presently ran away, and Pauline went into the house to get some crumbs for a tame pigeon who came from a neighboring house every day to be fed and petted by the little maiden. His feathers glimmered in the morning light, and Pauline stroked them gently with her delicate fingers as she gave him pieces of bread.

"I wonder if pigeons are ever thinking of anything," she said to herself reflectively. "This one must remember that he gets bread here or he wouldn't come. If I didn't give him any, perhaps he wouldn't come any more."

Pauline often held curious conversations with her nurse, who was a Presbyterian. She was fond of Pauline in her own way, and the little girl from long habit was much attached to her.

"Rebecca," said Pauline to her in the nursery—it was the evening of that very day when the street-boys had reproached her with having a nurse—"you don't like Holy Mary?"

"How do you know that?" growled Rebecca, who affected to be very busy searching in the bureau for something. She had never spoken of religion to the child, as Mrs. Archer had made this an express condition of her remaining after Pauline reached the age of reason.

"Rebecca," continued Pauline solemnly, "if you go to heaven, you'll *have* to see her up there."

"Hurry, now, and get undressed," said the

nurse, who was anxious to change the subject.

But Pauline was in an argumentative mood.

"I'm afraid perhaps you won't go to heaven at all," she said, "because you never go to Confession."

"You're the plaguiest child," said the nurse, "talking about sich things when you ought to be asleep."

"It would be awful to go into hell-fire," said the child. This was a quaint expression which she had picked up from the nurse herself. "So you'd better go to Confession."

With this parting shot, Pauline knelt down to say her prayers, and the nurse was very soon free to descend to the kitchen with her budget of complaint.

"Land's sake, what a child!" she observed to the cook. "She sends a cold shiver down my back with her talk. She's the most outlandish one to take care of. She's 'most always in good humor, 'cept once in a way she gets a bad turn; but she makes me creep with them big eyes of hers lookin' straight into you."

"Oh, it's herself has the purty face," said the cook, with whom Pauline was a special favorite.

"Yes, she's mighty pretty," said the nurse with a kind of professional pride; "not that she seems to set any store by her good looks."

"I'm afeard it's too good for this world she is," said the cook.

"Oh, she'll grow out of all that," said the housemaid; "lots o' them are just like that at the start. But I must say she's got a sweet way about her."

From that time forth, Pauline talked no more about religion in the nursery; for, having repeated the conversation to her mother, who was the gentlest, the most refined and long-suffering of invalids, that lady forbade her to renew the subject.

"My dear," she said, "you must not talk religion to your nurse. I have forbidden her to mention the subject to you, and so you see it is unfair that you should say anything to hurt her feelings."

Pauline thought for a moment before she answered:

"I only told her that perhaps she wouldn't go to heaven. I didn't say she would go into hell-fire, but only that it would be awful to go there."

Mrs. Archer could hardly keep from laughing, but she said gravely:

"I think you made your meaning very plain indeed, and I feel sorry for your nurse."

Pauline was sorry, too, when she thought of it in this light. She disliked nothing so much as hurting anybody's feelings. But what could she do? She hardly thought it would be right to assure Rebecca that she could go to heaven without Confession. So she wisely dropped the subject, and spent a very pleasant evening with her doll, to whom she could speak as freely as she chose, without fear of wounding its susceptibilities.

CHAPTER II.

PAULINE'S FATHER.

PAULINE could see her mother only at intervals. The doctor permitted but few and brief visits to the invalid, while her father, a very busy man, was not often in the house. Sometimes Pauline met him on the stairs that summer, and it seemed to surprise him that he could no longer toss her on his shoulder or ride her on his knee, as he had been accustomed to do in her earlier years.

"Hello!" he usually said. "What a big girl you have grown, to be sure! I must take you for a drive one of these Sundays."

But when Sunday came, popular Reginald Archer had one engagement or another, and this promise was neglected. One glorious September afternoon, however, when the people were just about beginning to come back to town after the summer, Mr. Archer found himself with nothing in particular to do. As he walked restlessly about the house, he chanced to catch sight of Pauline, and it struck him as quite a new idea that she was both pretty and distinguished-looking.

"Would you like to come out on the avenue for a walk with me?" he called out to her.

Pauline was delighted at the suggestion, though she felt rather shy of this big, bearded man whom she saw so seldom.

"Well, get on your toggery, then, and come along," Mr. Archer said carelessly, while Pauline hastened up to the nursery to get ready.

"It's about time he took some notice of her," grumbled the censorious Rebecca. "Half the time she might as well have no pa."

Pauline, coming out upon the avenue at her father's side, was sensible at once of the great rush of life and movement. The sound of the carriage-wheels and the horses' hoofs upon the pavement, the swift passing of handsome equipages, the hum of voices, and the stream of well-dressed people, all gave the impression of a panorama. Pauline was vaguely pleased with the wonderful costumes that she saw. Something in the little soul within her responded to everything that was beautiful in life. Her father, who knew a great many of the people and was constantly taking off his hat, was secretly proud of the small figure by his side. Engrossed as he was by the rise and fall of stocks, by coupons and dividends, he had a sixth sense, almost, for what was refined and pleasing in womankind. He could not bear anything loud or coarse about them, and it was because of this feeling that he had chosen for his wife the sweet and refined woman who now lay, as he feared, slowly dying in the dimness and solitude of her chamber. Pauline's costume was charming, simple and fresh, and worn with that indescribable air of daintiness which the child always gave to her clothes. Her father was very much gratified by the admiring looks cast upon his daughter, and the whispers which reached him of: "Isn't she lovely? Perfectly sweet!"

But Pauline was quite unconscious of it all. She walked along at her father's side erect and graceful as a willow, with her blue eyes looking into the mysterious something that always seemed before them.

"I suppose we may as well go to church," said her father in his indifferent way. "Would you care to?"

Pauline nodded.

"Yes, papa," she said softly.

But she was somewhat disappointed when he turned away from the avenue. She had expected that they were going into the glorious white cathedral, that always reminded her of heaven, and where the music had often thrilled her whole being. They walked eastward for a block or two, and reached an edifice comparatively plain and unadorned exteriorly. Pauline paused a moment at the foot of the steps, while her father called to her from the top rather impatiently:

"I thought you wanted to come in."

It cost Pauline an effort to ask the question which struggled to her lips. But her conscience was always on the alert, and she felt that she ought to ask it.

"Papa," said she hesitatingly, "is it a Catholic church?"

"Why, of course, little goose," he said, looking at her in surprise; and then, laughing: "Do you think I would take you anywhere else?"

The exterior of the church had struck Pauline as unfamiliar, and although she knew that her father was a Catholic, and probably thought him a much better one than he really was, still it had vaguely occurred to her that he might be going in just to see this as she thought Protestant church, and she was unwilling to accompany him.

She mounted the steps with alacrity when her father had given the assurance that all was right, while he said, with a laugh and another sharp look at her:

"I see you are an iron-bound bigot, Miss Pauline Archer."

The little girl did not at all understand what was meant by the words, but, the church door being now opened, the pealing of the organ and the lights upon the altar showed that Benediction was begun, and this drove the matter from her mind.

"This is St. Agnes' Church," whispered the father as they both took holy water. He said it with a view to remove the last trace of doubt from her mind; but the altar, with the sacred Host exposed upon it, would have done that.

Pauline knew all about St. Agnes, too, and the story recurred to her mind, filling it with a strange awe, as she seemed to realize what that Christian faith was for which that

maiden of the olden time had died. The
Benediction over, she walked home in her
quiet fashion, not saying a word to her father
of the thoughts which occupied her mind.
Few people imagine how secretive is much of
the life of childhood, how many thoughts are
suppressed, how many fancies remain unconjectured, even, by the prosaic elders.

That evening Reginald Archer said to his
wife:

"What a strange little creature Pauline is!"

"How do you mean, Reginald?" asked
Mrs. Archer somewhat anxiously.

He told her what had occurred, and how
Pauline had been unwilling to enter the
church until she was assured it was a Catholic
one. The mother smiled:

"She is a thorough little Catholic, at all
events, and I am glad of it; aren't you,
Reginald?"

"Oh, of course," he assented absently; "but
I do think the mite has been too much alone.
She has some odd, old-fashioned ways about
her."

Mrs. Archer sighed.

"I fear so," she said, "and it saddens me,
for I am so helpless."

"Don't fret about it," said the husband; "we'll see what can be done. Her cousins are coming home earlier this year, and we'll try and have her with them, for one thing. But, by Jove!" he added emphatically, "she is awfully pretty, Ada. Half the women on the avenue looked admiringly at her."

"I am not sure that beauty isn't a fatal gift for a woman," said Mrs. Archer doubtfully.

"Nonsense, dear! it's worth more than a fortune to her," said Reginald in his off-hand way. "Why, you yourself were just the prettiest creature possible when I saw you first."

"My beauty, such as it was," said Mrs. Archer, a little wistfully, "hasn't lasted very long."

Reginald Archer scanned his wife's sadly worn and wasted face before he replied cheerily:

"When you get strong again, you'll be all right."

"If I ever do," she exclaimed almost involuntarily; for, though she said little about it, it was a fact borne in upon her constantly that the crowning gift of strength was never to be hers on this bright, glorious earth.

From that day forth, and following upon that conversation, there was a gradual change in Pauline Archer's life.

Her father began to occupy himself seriously with her. In the first place, it gratified the vanity of this self-absorbed and somewhat Mammon-worshipping stock-broker to have so pretty a daughter, and one who bore the hall-mark of birth and breeding even in the quaint simplicity of her manner and despite her shyness. Then he was very fond of her in his own fashion, and began to understand that she must have rather a lonely time of it. He told her that her cousins were expected home very soon, and that that event would make things pleasanter for her.

"But perhaps I'll be so ashamed I won't want to speak to them," said Pauline to her nurse, when she had repeated what her father had told her.

"If ever I heard of sich an outlandish child!" said the nurse, holding up her hands in protest. "Ashamed to speak to her own kin!"

The Archers were not as wealthy as they had been, owing to some daring speculations on the part of Reginald which had resulted disastrously, so that they no longer lived in the very heart of the fashionable world, and some of their acquaintances were mildly dismayed to find them located rather far west and somewhat out of the charmed circle. This was one of the reasons why Pauline had not associated very much with other children. The Archers' immediate circle of friends lived mostly at some distance, and were content to visit and invite them at intervals, so that there was little opportunity for Pauline to form an intimacy with the children of those families. Another and more powerful reason was to be found in Mrs. Archer's unworldly notions and her dread of exposing Pauline to indiscriminate companionship.

"When I am not there to watch over her," she used to say, "it makes me doubly anxious; and neither wealth nor high position is a guarantee that a child is a fit associate for my poor little Pauline."

Pauline sometimes heard her father say that they were poor. Of course he only meant it in a comparative degree, for the Archers lived very comfortably indeed, and the head of the house spent considerable on himself. In fact, since they had been living quietly, he had recouped some of his losses and was in a fair way to recover lost ground. Of course they no longer kept carriages or horses, and even before Mrs. Archer had become a confirmed invalid she had been somewhat limited as to elegant costumes and costly entertainments.

"I am certain that reverses are good for people," she had said to her husband. "It helps one to escape what sometimes degenerates into the vulgarity of wealth, and far graver dangers even than that."

Her husband, who did not believe that wealth could ever be an evil, looked at her inquiringly.

"I mean, of course, in a spiritual way," she said. "One hardens towards his fellow men, one loses sight of his own lowliness before God, and grows attached to the world and its glitter."

Reginald patted her cheek.

"No amount of wealth could make you do all that," he said cheerfully.

"No one can answer for herself," said she thoughtfully; but she did not pursue the subject, and Reginald was presently off to buy and sell, to struggle and wrestle, as if wealth were "the one thing necessary."

CHAPTER III.

LITTLE MARY KELLY.

PAULINE, who had her own thoughts upon the subject, said one day to her nurse:

"I don't think we're poor at all, but little Mary Kelly is."

"Little Mary Kelly!" echoed the nurse. "Who in the land's name is she?"

"Her father fixes shoes," Pauline said quietly. "I saw him tacking and hammering and doing like this."

Pauline imitated the man's action so exactly that the nurse said with a sniff, but with some real curiosity:

"A cobbler! But how came you, missy, to know that he had a child, or what her name was?"

"I saw the boys chasing her to-day," said Pauline, "and I was sorry for her, because they call me names, and perhaps they would chase me only I am bigger and live in this house. Then I heard one boy say:

"'There! now she's down.'

"'Who?' said another.

"'Little Mary Kelly, and I guess she's killed. The cops will be coming, and we'd better scoot.'"

To the wonder of her nurse, Pauline repeated the words just as she had heard them, winding up, as she so often did, with a question:

"What's 'cops'? When they said they were coming I looked all around, but 1 couldn't see anything."

"Never you mind what they are," said the nurse, "and don't you be picking up words from street-boys."

"After the boys were gone," said Pauline, "I went over to the little girl. She had fallen down and cut her nose, and it was bleeding a great deal."

Pauline turned rather pale at the remembrance, as she had when the sight first met her eyes. But she proceeded:

"She was crying very hard, and she didn't seem to have any handkerchief, so that her frock was getting all stained. I gave her mine. It was quite clean, Rebecca, and I think she was glad to get it."

"It's a wonder you made up your mind to speak to any one," said the nurse.

"I didn't like to, very much," admitted Pauline, "but she was very little and I *had* to, for fear she might bleed to death."

"No danger! But what did you do next?" said the nurse. "Did you get back your handkerchief?"

"Oh, no," said Pauline with a shudder, remembering the stain upon it. "I told the little girl that she'd better go home, and I would go with her in case the boys came back. She was glad, I think. But I wouldn't have been much use if they had come," she wound up with a laugh.

"You're right there," Rebecca said, "and I just do wonder what you'd have done if they had come."

"I think I'd have stood still and looked at them and held little Mary's hand," said Pauline. "But I don't know; perhaps I'd have run away."

"You took the young one home, anyhow?" inquired Rebecca, her curiosity again gaining the mastery.

"Yes, she lived a block away," said Pauline. "I walked beside her, and all of a sudden she went down into a cellar. I looked in, and I saw a man fixing shoes there, and she called out to him, so I suppose he was her father."

After this recital Pauline stood still pondering, and knitting her brows till they met. At last she exclaimed:

"It must be awful, Rebecca, to live in a cellar!"

"Well, be thankful you haven't got to do it," returned the nurse shortly, "and keep away from sich places and people."

But Pauline's mother, on hearing the story, said:

"You did quite right, dear, and I shall tell Rebecca to go with you in the morning to ask if the little girl is quite well again, and you may take her some candy or fruit, if you like."

"I might be ashamed to give it to her," observed Pauline.

"You needn't be; but in any case Rebecca won't mind."

Pauline went to sleep that night with a curious, excited feeling. She thought it was something strange and new and a little bit awful to go down into a cellar, but with Rebecca's support it could be managed. Besides, her mother seemed to wish it, and she really wanted to go herself.

Next morning, Rebecca, who had her own thoughts about the proposed expedition, but was too well trained to express them in opposition to her mistress's orders, helped Pauline to dress, in no very good humor.

"I particularly want Pauline to see something of the poor and know something of their lives," Mrs. Archer had said. "There is such danger, in these big, God-forgetting cities, of a child growing up to despise the poor and regard only the rich."

Rebecca had made no answer. She felt that her mistress was thinking aloud rather than speaking to her; and besides she could not follow such reasoning at all, and put it down to a "sick body's notions." Poverty was in Rebecca's eyes, if not a disgrace, at least something to be ashamed of, and her long residence in the families of the rich had made her almost forget that she was of the poor herself.

Guided by Pauline, Rebecca finally arrived at the head of the cellar steps, where the little girl paused with natural timidity, as well as a delicacy which made her fear to intrude.

"Perhaps they won't like it," she whispered.

But Rebecca, who was troubled with no such scruples and wanted to get the visit over as soon as possible, went briskly down, calling Pauline to come after her. Before they had reached the foot of the steps, a small figure suddenly emerged from the comparative gloom beyond and, catching sight of Pauline, ran back hastily. As she went, she cried out to some one in the background:

"Daddy! daddy! it's the little lady. Come and see."

Pauline, hearing this, advanced into the cellar, and the cobbler, standing up, received her with a politeness none the less genuine for being unpolished. Rebecca, however, did the talking.

"This young lady's mother sent her to know how your little girl is to-day," said Rebecca with the air of superiority she always assumed in dealing with the poor.

"My little girl," repeated the cobbler, as if he did not quite understand.

"Was she very much hurt when she fell

down yesterday?" asked Pauline, her shyness yielding to her desire to seem friendly.

"Oh, no, miss, she was more frightened than hurt," said the cobbler. "But you must be the little lady that she said picked her up and came home with her."

"Yes, I came home with her," said Pauline.

"Ah, then, miss, dear, and I'm entirely obliged to you," said the man, with an emotion which made his young guest feel uncomfortable, "as well as the kind thought you and your mother—God bless her, whoever she is, for a real lady—had in sending to ask."

"I was very sorry she got thrown down," Pauline continued.

"Oh, little miss," said the cobbler, with a smile on his grim visage, and a note in his voice which would have struck an older person as pathetic, "the children of the poor gets many hard knocks, but mebbe they don't feel them as others do."

All this while little Mary had been keeping in the background. Pauline did not like to look around much; it would have seemed very rude. But she thought the cellar a very strange place, with the cobbler's chair and bench in the centre of it, as well as his tools, while bits of leather were strewn all about. Boots and shoes in various stages of repair were visible, as well as a few great sheets of leather. In one corner was a play which little Mary had evidently been making on the floor, and Pauline's big blue eyes noted a few strips of the prevailing fabric, soft leather, some of which were colored, a penny doll with the paint off its face, and a couple of pinwheels.

"Come here, Mary," called the father, "and thank the little lady for coming to ask after you."

As Mary came out from behind her father's chair, half-pleased and half-shy, Pauline could not help noticing that her pinafore was torn and that her hands were not very clean.

"But it must be hard to keep clean down here," she said to herself, "and she's too little to mend her pinafore. I'm clean, but then I have a nurse."

Pauline offered little Mary the parcel of candy which she had brought, as well as a parcel of bananas. Mary was so overcome that she forgot any longer to be bashful.

"Oh, what lovely candy—and those!" she said, holding up a banana to her father.

"I'm sure it's very kind of you, miss," said the cobbler, who seemed really touched by the whole affair. "And it isn't too much kindness my motherless little one gets. I just have to keep her mostly with myself. For, when she goes out, you see the rough handling she's liable to get. I'm afeard, too, of bad company for her."

Pauline looked with new interest at the little girl who had no mother, and only this dark cellar to play in, near her father, who was always at work.

"Perhaps," said Pauline with a kindly impulse, "you might let her come up near our house sometimes. It's generally quiet there, and if any rough children came, I could call Rebecca."

It was just as well that worthy woman did not hear this last proposition, or she might have vetoed it on the spot and mortally offended the cobbler. But she was already on the steps above, waiting impatiently for her charge, and intent meanwhile in watching what was going on in that busy thoroughfare of Eighth Avenue.

It was pretty to observe Pauline's manner towards the cobbler and his little daughter, so gravely, punctiliously polite was she, and, more than that, warming into a cordiality and kindliness which she might not have shown to people of her own station.

"God bless you for your goodness," said the man, looking down with a strangely softened expression upon his visitor. "I'm afeard my little Mary's no playfellow for the likes of you, and mebbe your folks wouldn't like it."

Pauline did not know what answer to make to this remark, but she said presently:

"I think little Mary will like it up there, and I will show her some dolls and things and let her feed the pigeon."

"Oh, may I go to feed the pigeon?" said little Mary, quite overcome by this last temptation, which appealed to her with special force.

"But mebbe your folks might object," said the cobbler.

"Oh, I know my mother will be pleased," said Pauline, "and my father won't mind at all."

"Well, I'll send her up, then, some morning, soon," said the man, "but be sure to send her home if she's in the way."

The poor man was divided between a desire

to give his little daughter pleasure and a fear that she might be intruding upon these people of another world.

"Well, good-by," said Pauline as Rebecca called impatiently for her to come. Her eyes rested first on the cobbler and then wandered to little Mary.

As she turned away the cobbler looked earnestly after the small figure, which had never looked more dainty or more elegant than in these dingy surroundings.

"There's not many like her," he said, returning to his stitching and tacking, while Mary crept close to his side.

"P'raps she's one of the fairies you told me about," said she; "her hair shines and she wears lovely clothes."

"She's better than that," said the cobbler; and Mary, going back to her play, wondered what better there could be than a fairy except the people in heaven. Like Pauline, this little girl was sometimes lonely. Her father's companionship was the only one she had. For he would not suffer her to mingle with the rough boys and almost as unmanageable girls who frequented the neighborhood. He was striving in that darksome cellar, in so far as he could, to bring Mary up as some precious flower.

He stopped his work a moment to look wistfully at her, where she sat on the floor with her play, unconscious of all that was lacking in her life. She was playing, quite happily, that her doll was the little lady who had come with candy.

"God help her!" said the father to himself. His mind was busy pondering whether or not it was wisest to let Mary accept Pauline's invitation. If she did, it might only dissatisfy her by giving her an insight into a life different from her own, and moreover she might meet with some slight from "that stuck-up servant," as he mentally named Rebecca, or from others. On the other hand, it seemed cruel to refuse his Mary the offered gleam of sunshine, and surely "the little lady wasn't stuck up, anyhow."

Thus he argued with his own heart, so that when the twilight came that day the cobbler, stitching hard to finish the mending of a shoe by the waning light, was thinking of Pauline, about whom little Mary was prattling close by and invoking blessings on her head, at the very time that Mrs. Archer, at the close of one more day of pain and weariness, was rousing herself to interest in the recital of Pauline's experience.

"Isn't it strange," said Pauline; "she's so small and she hasn't got any mother."

Pauline's eyes were gazing out of the window thoughtfully. Mrs. Archer, with a quick pang, wondered if some one might not shortly be saying the very same thing of her little Pauline. "If I can but live till she is grown up!" she said within herself. "Dear Lord, if it be Thy will!"

She quite approved of the invitation Pauline had given the cobbler's child to play upon their steps and sidewalk under Rebecca's protection. She also made up her mind that after suitable inquiry had been made as to the child's character and disposition she would go farther, and permit Pauline to invite her into the house and plan various little pleasures for her.

"What, in the name of mercy, have you got here?" said Reginald Archer on the following morning, almost stumbling over little Mary as he came out of the dark hall into the sunshine.

"It's little Mary Kelly," said Pauline gravely.

"Oh, indeed! Well, I'm not much wiser than I was before, but I think it's the first time I ever saw you playing with any child."

After he had stepped into the hansom which, at his telephone summons, had driven up to the door, he called Pauline.

"Who's the little girl?" he asked.

"She belongs to the cobbler," said Pauline solemnly.

Reginald Archer exploded in a great, hearty laugh and thrust his hand into his pocket.

"Oh, that's who she is! So you've got to treat her well. Here's a quarter to buy some sweet stuff."

Kissing Pauline in his careless fashion, and with a droll glance at the diminutive figure which was seated demurely on the steps, the busy broker gave an order to the cabman and was driven away.

After that little Mary Kelly became an institution, a plaything rather than a playfellow, one who listened, without understanding, to Pauline's quaint sayings. She never quite got over the notion that her benefactress might have some connection with that fairy world of which her father, with his vein of Celtic poetry and imagination, had given her an insight.

CHAPTER IV.

AN UNEXPECTED PLEASURE.

One afternoon when Reginald Archer had nothing very particular to do and was feeling somewhat bored, he began to remember his good resolutions with regard to his daughter and the promises which he had made in that connection to his wife. It occurred to him that he would take Pauline to the Park and show her some of the sights. So he put his head out of the window of the library, where he was sitting, to see if Pauline was at her customary post upon the steps. Yes, Pauline was there with little Mary Kelly beside her, both intent on feeding the pigeon with crumbs.

"If you touch him just there where his feathers are so very purple," Pauline was saying, "it feels as if he was made of silk."

"P'raps he is," said Mary, struck by the idea and looking up into Pauline's face.

"Oh, no," said Pauline, "feathers are different from silk."

"Are they?" asked little Mary, who didn't know very much about either.

"I wonder if he knows when we're talking about him," said Pauline.

Mary eyed the pigeon closely, but got no information from him on the subject. The bird seemed chiefly intent on picking up the crumbs as speedily as possible. In fact, it was plain that he didn't care very much whether they were talking about him or not.

"If he could speak," added Pauline, "I wonder what he would say."

"Birds can't speak, though," said Mary, feeling that this was something she did know about.

"Some kinds can," said Pauline.

"Can they?" asked Mary, in astonishment.

"Parrots and some others, I think. I don't remember their names," said Pauline.

Here Mr. Archer's head came altogether out of the window, and he called out:

"Pauline, would you like to go up to the Park with me this afternoon?"

Pauline nodded her head several times to show her great pleasure at the idea. Then she paused with a hesitating glance at the figure of the child beside her.

"That can be managed, too, I think," said her father. "Your distinguished friend can go with us, only Rebecca will have to tidy you both up somewhat."

He meant this latter remark especially for the visitor, for Pauline, as usual, was as dainty as if she had come out of the traditional bandbox. Poor little Mary, on the other hand, despite her father's efforts, was wofully shabby.

"Although you haven't answered," said Mr. Archer, "except by nodding your head like a mandarin, I take it that you want to go. So I shall ring for Rebecca."

He did so, and having given her a few instructions, she took the children away with her to the nursery, grumbling and dissatisfied at heart. She told herself that she had no patience with the freaks of rich people. They were always doing outlandish things and making trouble for themselves and others.

"I'm sure I never seen the like," she soliloquized. "Children out of slums being made welcome and taken out to the Park, if you please!"

Nevertheless she presently transformed little Mary. She put on her a discarded frock and pinafore of Pauline's which that little lady had worn at an early age. These, with the addition of a hat which had once shaded Pauline's blue eyes, set upon hair which Rebecca had vigorously brushed, caused the child to present a very respectable appearance indeed. She stood very much in awe of Mr. Archer, and bent down her head when he spoke to her till her lately brushed hair fell over her face.

However, she was very soon relieved from embarrassment, for, once they had boarded a Broadway cable-car, Mr. Archer left the children to themselves. He went out upon the platform, and stood there in conversation with an acquaintance whom he met. And even after they reached their destination he said very little to Pauline and nothing at all to her playmate, except a careless word or two.

Little Mary Kelly had never before been taken to the Park. Her father had thought of taking her there from time to time, but even car-fare is a consideration to the very poor, so he had always consoled himself with the idea that when Mary was big enough to walk they would go up some Sunday. And he could not restrain a slight feeling of disappointment when he heard, later on, that Mary had been taken to that wonderful place by others than himself.

Even the ride in the cars, short as it was, was a novelty to little Mary, who sat very still, with a broad smile of delight brightening her face. It was an added enjoyment to Pauline to notice the joy of her tiny playmate, and that evening she communicated the result of her observations to her nurse and her mother.

"She never saw the Park," said Pauline to her nurse, " and never flowers growing, in her whole life before."

"Of course not," snapped Rebecca, who disapproved altogether of the new acquaintance. "Where would sich a child see flowers? Not in her father's cellar, I suppose."

"She thought the swans were fairies, and the lake an enchanted place," Pauline continued, adding thoughtfully: "She seems to know more about fairies than almost anything else."

"It would be better for her to know saving truths," said Rebecca with a sanctimonious air, "than all those lies."

"Are fairies lies?" asked Pauline, opening her eyes wide. She had been taught to have so great a horror of falsehood that this new idea jarred upon her.

"Of course they is," said the nurse. "This beggar-child ought to be taught gospel truth."

"She doesn't beg," corrected Pauline gently, "and she knows her prayers very well, and goes to church almost every day, although she's so little."

Rebecca sniffed. It would have pleased her better had the little girl from the cellar been an actual heathen. It would have fitted in better with her idea of heaven, too, which she vaguely thought ought to be reserved for respectable people, who were either of independent fortune or, at least, earning good wages.

Pauline did not pursue the subject. Rebecca's bitterness scarcely touched her; she did not understand it, and it hardly occurred to her to wonder why Rebecca was always cross when little Mary was mentioned.

This conversation of course took place after the children's return from their expedition; but the following chapter will be devoted to the account of their afternoon at the Park, what they did and saw there, and how little Mary enjoyed it.

CHAPTER V.

THE AFTERNOON AT THE PARK.

LITTLE Mary Kelly was in a very ecstasy of delight from the moment that she followed Mr. Archer and Pauline in at the Fifth Avenue gate of Central Park till they left it in the glow of the setting sun. There was the band playing on the Mall, which was full of people—men, women, and children—walking about or sitting on the benches. There was the smooth, velvety grass, varied from time to time by flower-beds and trees of all varieties, the latter meeting overhead at times; there were rocks grown over with creeping plants; curious tunnels, and delightful summer-houses, and the lake, which to little Mary's eyes might have been a sea, so broad it was. Surely it was one of those enchanted places of which her father had told her, and the swans its fairies. She looked at them with something like awe as they glided along over the smooth water, so white, so graceful.

"Oh, ain't they lovely!" she whispered to Pauline.

"Yes, they go along so softly and gracefully," said Pauline.

Presently Mr. Archer hailed a swan-boat and put the two children into it, asking the boatman to look after them a bit while he sat down in the shade of a tree to smoke a cigar.

Once out upon the water, little Mary was at the height of blissful wonderment and enjoyment. She looked often at Pauline, who sat erect and demure, her big blue eyes, with their long lashes, shadowed by the leaf of her leghorn, with its simple but elegant trimming, which finished the dainty costume of zephyr gingham enlivened by pretty ribbons. To Mary's infantile mind recurred her first idea that Pauline might be a fairy or even the queen of the fairies, who commanded all those beautiful white creatures that floated around them.

Pauline was thinking her own tranquil thoughts meanwhile, which were often deeper and truer than those of most children of her age. They touched the why and wherefore, the inner heart of things. She was wondering just then about the swans, if they knew how beautiful they were, and if they ever talked among themselves, or ever went down into silver caverns, as the story-books said they did. She saw the shadows of the drooping trees reflected, and it occurred to her that those old tales might be true about other cities lying buried under the waters.

"If the boat were to sink and we went down there," she thought, "perhaps we'd see a lot of strange things."

She watched little Mary's chubby dark face framed in its bush of dark hair and forming such a contrast to her own—though that she did not realize. She saw the little fat hands clasped every once in a while as the child gave utterance to cries of delight or began to croon songs, which caused the stolid boatman to stare curiously at her. Once or twice he spoke to her.

"Look out," he said, "or you'll go overboard. Don't you lean over there, or the fishes will have you."

These remonstrances, though not addressed to her, made Pauline uncomfortable. The man's presence in the boat had been a restraint on her, keeping her silent, and she thought that she would just hate it if he turned round and spoke to her. Little Mary did not mind the man or his speech, but she was very much disturbed at the idea of the cold slimy fishes " having her "; though, indeed, her only knowledge of those creatures was the seeing them exposed for sale at a fish-market or brought home to be cooked by her father. So she shrank as far away as possible from the edge of the boat, which presently reached the landing after a complete tour of the lake.

Mr. Archer called out from the shore to the children:

" I suppose you've had about enough of that. So get out now, and you may have a drive in the goat-carriages and perhaps a donkey-ride, if you care about it."

Urged by these alluring promises, the two little people stepped quickly ashore, after one wistful glance at the water they were leaving. They were presently being driven up and down by solemn-faced jehus, to whom the raptures of their childish customers were as the joy of mortals before the gods.

Pauline's face was beaming with smiles, and little Mary Kelly laughed aloud with such unaffected glee that her infectious merriment seized upon Mr. Archer. It was a new experience to him, this giving pleasure to others. Indeed, it is an enjoyment in which the rich far too seldom indulge. They forget how few and simple are the pleasures of the poor, and how easy it is to add to them.

Reginald Archer had always been very good and devoted to his wife, and before she had become an invalid he had taken her to various places of amusement, spending money lavishly, but not always realizing that, though his gentle companion strove hard to enjoy what he enjoyed, her physical ailments made it very difficult and wearisome for her. He had been kind and indulgent to Pauline when she crossed his path. But until the last few weeks he had totally neglected her.

So here he found himself providing pleasures that were an unmixed delight to these two simple beings. Pauline was the happier that her little playfellow was so overjoyed. For Mary it was as a sun rising on her dismal horizon which would never entirely go down. Its light would illumine the cellar for a long time to come.

The drive in the goat-wagons was followed by a few turns up and down on the back of the patient donkeys that stood waiting, saddled and bridled, for just such riders. These animals, having received an impetus from the driver, trotted off after their peculiar fashion. A man ran beside, and in little Mary's case held her on, while Pauline sat upright, the sun making glints in her hair where it fell waving over her shoulders, and her eyes looking away into the distance with that look which her nurse called "creepy."

She stroked the donkey's head gently as she got down, and the animal, appreciating her soft touch strove to thrust his rough head and long ears towards her again.

"Queen Mab and Bottom," said the father, who had just been seeing the "Midsummernight's Dream" at Daly's.

"Who is Bottom?" inquired Pauline.

"Oh, the fellow that put on the ass's head," said her father vaguely, "and you were Mab, Queen of the Fairies."

Little Mary caught this speech, and it confirmed her more than ever in the idea about Pauline.

"We must see if we can get some ice-cream now," said Mr. Archer, "unless either of you objects."

"I don't think we will," said Pauline with her quaint little laugh, and Mr. Archer hailed a Park omnibus. He had never driven in this vehicle before, but it was a day of new experiences, and he told the driver to let them off near the Casino. They were soon seated at a marble table, with pink-and-white ices and a heaping plate of cake before them. Little Mary, still shy of Mr. Archer, stuck her finger in her mouth and would not begin to eat until that good-natured gentleman, guessing what the trouble was and not caring to take ices himself, as he was smoking, moved off to some distance. He lazily watched the two, thinking how the dark, gypsy-like face of the cobbler's child set off that of his dainty Pauline, who ate slowly and sparingly, with that peculiar grace she lent to every action. She helped little Mary before herself to cake, choosing out the very nicest ones for her. Mary had never tasted ice-cream before, and the coldness of it puzzled her at first, but, encouraged by Pauline's example, she took to it very kindly, and soon made an end of the pink-and-white mound.

"We'll take a stroll down to the animals,"

said Mr. Archer next, "and after that we'll move homewards."

So they went down to the enclosures where the deer were kept. Mild-eyed fawns came to the railing and thrust out their heads to be petted. Pauline, who had a natural sympathy with all living things and seemed to draw them towards her, stroked their heads, accompanying her action with softly spoken, endearing words, while little Mary looked on with breathless interest. The great stags, with shining horns, held aloof in their stately fashion, and Pauline, looking at them, said to her companion:

"Mamma told me that once there was a saint who went out hunting—I think it was before he was a saint, perhaps; and just when he was going to shoot the deer, he saw a cross between its horns. So he didn't kill that one, and he never shot any more."

"What's a deer?" whispered Mary.

"That," said Pauline; and Mary, openmouthed, looked at the tall stag, with its wonderful horns, upon which Pauline also fixed her blue eyes, saying:

"Aren't horns strange? It must be terrible to have such heavy ones on your head."

Pauline took little Mary's hand as Mr. Archer hurried them on to the monkey-house, where the smaller child laughed so explosively that Mr. Archer almost thought of suppressing her, as he said, but it was a pity to spoil sport, and, after all, what did it matter?

"That's a very old one over there," said Pauline in her slow, deliberate speech. "Perhaps he's a hundred."

"There's a tiny little one," said Mary. "Aren't their faces just hideous? They look like dirty old men."

One of the monkeys put out a long paw and seized a lock of Mary's hair, pulling out two or three hairs, which he seemed to examine curiously. Mary screamed with delight, her laugh, with its ringing cadence, being heard all over the building, and provoking many a smile from the bystanders.

"She's having a good time and no mistake," said a man in passing Mr. Archer.

"There's no doubt about that," replied Reginald Archer genially.

The elephants were even a greater joy to both the little girls. What child, in the history of the world, hasn't loved elephants? Their huge stature and bulk, their funny, twinkling eyes, lost in fat, but yet so wise and far-seeing, their ever-active trunk, are forever fascinating to the tiny mortals, who stand before them as ants in presence of those great moving mountains. Mr. Archer had brought from the restaurant where they had eaten ice-cream a few apples and nuts. He knew it would amuse his young companions to bestow those upon the mighty beasts, that rejoiced in such things as though they were so many school-boys. The result was that he found it rather hard to get Pauline and Mary away from the delightful performance. The elephant's trunk found its way into each of their pockets in turn, and deftly produced thence a few nuts or half an apple.

But at last they had to say good-by to the elephants, and hurry on past foxes and peccaries and growling bears and wolves and leopards and hyenas and giraffes, till they came to the tigers and lions. At the very moment of their approach one of the largest of the monarchs of the forest slowly raised himself and, lashing his tail, gave vent to a fearful roar, which shook the enclosure and was echoed up among the neighboring rocks. Little Mary hid her face in Pauline's skirts and wept. She seemed to think that the roar was specially addressed to her, and the sight of the terrible animal in his rage filled her with terror.

Pauline stood erect before him, her blue eyes half closed in her intent gaze, which the beast returned uneasily, beginning to pace up and down in disquietude. Pauline was charmed by the great flowing mane and noble pose, and was not at all afraid of him. She tried to comfort Mary.

"He isn't angry at us," she said. "He must have got angry at something before we came, because we didn't go very near him or do anything to him."

It tickled Reginald Archer's sense of humor to think of tiny Mary or diminutive Pauline rousing the lion to fury.

"Very likely he's hungry," he said briefly.

"Probably he is," said Pauline thoughtfully; and she said afterwards to Mary that she was rather glad he wasn't angry at them, even though he couldn't get out.

"He's ter'ble," said little Mary, venturing, however, another look at him, but swiftly hiding her face again.

"He looks a good deal like a king," said

Pauline, "a very great king. I'm sure he liked it a great deal better when he was in the forest than in a cage. It must be awful to be in a cage. And even when he wants to roar, so many people hear him."

This thought seemed peculiarly distasteful to Pauline as she followed her father silently in the direction of the hippopotamuses. Little Mary held on very tight to Pauline's hand, looking back every once in a while to be sure that the lion wasn't after them. When they reached the edge of the artificial pond, the keepers were trying to drive the huge beasts up out of the water to be fed. Little Mary was rather disposed to be afraid of these, too, with their uncouth forms and discordant grunts. But after a time she became, like Pauline, interested in observing the efforts of the men to make them come to the surface.

"Oh, there's his back now!" cried she in glee, as the keepers resorted to the device of letting the water out of the tank.

"I don't think he knows that the water's going out," observed Pauline; "he imagines there's plenty of it."

"There he is!" cried Mary, as one of the creatures went wobbling up the broad plank, grunting discontentedly. He was presently comforted, however, by pitchforkfuls of hay, thrust into his mouth by an attendant.

"It's a wonder he wouldn't rather stay up on land," said Pauline. "I'd just hate to live in the water; wouldn't you, Mary?"

Mary nodded her head several times to show her entire agreement with the sentiment.

"She has your trick of nodding," remarked Mr. Archer to Pauline. "I must buy you a mandarin that you may see how absurd it seems." He had begun to be a trifle weary of the day's sport, and looked at his watch frequently. He now suggested that it was time to take the car, and led the way towards one of the exits.

CHAPTER VI.

THE SAME STORY DIFFERENTLY TOLD.

That evening the cobbler and Mrs. Archer each received a version of the day's adventures. Through the thoughtfulness of the latter, Rebecca had been sent down that Mary's father might not be anxious about his daughter's long absence. So he sat there, listening to what Mary had to tell, as he stitched busily away at a pair of shoes, the payment for which was to buy their dinner for the morrow.

The child's description was necessarily imperfect and disjointed. She had few words at her command and could not remember the big ones, while she was ignorant of the names of many of the animals and other things she had seen. But there had been a time in the cobbler's life when he, a merry boy, had spent long, hilarious days there, playing with the zest of a healthy, cheerful lad. Of course there were many new attractions added to those which in his boyhood had made the Park "a joy forever," and he had never had money to go boating on the lake, or drive in the 'bus, or eat ice-cream. So that he could form an idea of all that Mary sought to tell, and enter into her feelings, as well as supply many a missing link. Big lions and tiny monkeys were freely mentioned, but Mary was wise enough not to try to call either the elephant or the hippopotamus by its name. The former she spoke of as the big, big one who put his tongue into her pocket, and the latter as another big one that lived in the water and didn't want to come up. The lake and the swans brought a sympathetic smile to the cobbler's face. Was it not one of his favorite amusements, long ago, to bring crumbs of bread to the Park to feed the big white swans? And although he heaved a sigh, too, as some of the boy's "long, long thoughts" came back to him, still it cheered him at his work to think of those pleasant things, and it gladdened him to know that little Mary had had one glorious day at least.

Pauline, too, by her story of that happy holiday afternoon brightened the gloom of her mother's invalid apartment. It brought pleasant memories to Mrs. Archer as she lay and listened. Like the cobbler, she, too, went back to the days of her youth, when she used to ride in the Park on a particular and dearly loved horse which her father had given her on her sixteenth birthday. This remembrance gave her a very much keener pleasure than the thought of the later times, when, reclining in the victoria, she had been borne along in the stream of fashion, a part of its panorama-like unreality. Unreal all, she reflected, though she said no word of this to Pauline, being unwilling to lessen the child's pleasure in the very slightest degree.

"And how did little Mary enjoy it?" Mrs. Archer inquired.

"Oh, she just loved it," said Pauline. "She had never been to a park before, and she thought at first it belonged to the fairies."

"So it does," said Mrs. Archer, smiling.

Pauline was puzzled. Of course her mother knew, but she did not think there were any real fairies, and she had heard her father say that the Park belonged to the city.

"The fairies of youth and happiness," explained Mrs. Archer.

"Oh," said Pauline, resuming her narrative. "We both put our feet on the grass, but we didn't walk there. I told Mary she mustn't, because she didn't know. So we only touched it. I wonder what makes it so green."

"The same Power that does all things in nature," said the invalid.

"God only showed the men how to make Central Park," reasoned Pauline.

"That's all," said Mrs. Archer. "But the best part of it is His own work. The men couldn't make trees or grass or flowers, nor place the sky overhead with its shining sun."

"Wouldn't it be queer if there was no sky?" said Pauline, trying to conjure up a picture in her own mind.

"Very queer indeed," said Mrs. Archer, laughing; "it would be something like a house without a roof, and a dark house at that. But tell me some more about your wonderful doings. I want to hear everything."

"We went to see the animals," said Pauline, "but not until after we had sailed around the lake, and ridden on the donkeys, and driven in the goat-carriages. The goats ran along very quickly with us; they didn't seem to find us very heavy. But the boys who were driving ran just as fast. Then we got ice-cream, and some time afterwards we began to go round the menagerie. We liked the elephants and monkeys best, but the lion was very proud and grand, and he roared very loud. It was terrible to hear him."

Pauline had not yet finished her detailed description of the various animals, when Mrs. Archer's attendants came to shut out the last glimpse of day and turn on the electric light, softly shaded for the invalid's tired eyes.

So Pauline went up to the nursery, where the story was continued, Rebecca listening, nothing loath, as curiosity was her particular weakness. Pauline embellished her narrative with additions which her innate sense of propriety had prevented her from giving in the sick-room. She was always gentle and quiet there, and spoke in her distinct but softly modulated voice. Mrs. Archer used to say that it rested her to have her near or hear her talk. So she reserved for her nurse's steady nerves, and ears attuned to nursery noises, an imitation of the various beasts, the growling of the bears, the laughing of the hyena, and even the roar of the lion.

"He went this way," she said, swelling out her chest, throwing back her head, and pulling out her hair to simulate a mane. When the turn of the hippopotamus came, Pauline gave so graphic an illustration of that huge animal crawling, tumbling, waddling up to the land and snatching mouthfuls of hay from the pitchfork that Rebecca at length begged her to stop.

"I've a'most split my sides laughin'," she said. "You stop, or you'll give me a right-down pain there."

Pauline was beginning to be rather tired herself, so she presently permitted Rebecca to help her to undress and to tuck her into bed.

"I wonder what it will be like up in heaven," Pauline said, with one of the sudden changes of mood that drove the prosaic nurse nearly to distraction. "But we'll only know when we're dead."

"Sich a child!" said Rebecca testily. She did not want to be reminded of such unpleasant truths. In reading her Bible she usually picked out what she called "the cheerfullest parts"—those that gave her a pleasant sense of her own righteousness and did not dwell too much on what was to come.

"Wait!" said Pauline, suddenly springing up, just as Rebecca had got her securely tucked in. "I forgot my new prayer to Holy Mary."

This was the *Memorare*, which she had but lately learned. She knelt at the foot of the bed, more than ever like an angel in her white gown and flowing hair, as she folded her hands and fixed her earnest eyes on the statue.

Rebecca turned away, moving about the room, opening and shutting drawers and keeping her back to Pauline, as she always did when the child was at prayer.

Pauline, standing up, gave a few touches to the vases of flowers which she had put upon the shelf in front of the statue that morning.

"I wonder if Holy Mary has stars for her crown up in heaven," she said.

"Oh, you're always wondering about something, and I wish you'd get into bed again."

Pauline did so, Rebecca repeating the ceremony of tucking her in with rather vicious jerks.

"Now don't you get up out of there for nothing," said the nurse.

"I won't get up again," promised Pauline. "Good-night, Rebecca."

The little voice sounded somewhat muffled from under the coverlet, and presently the nurse, bending over her charge, saw that the long lashes were lying softly on the fair cheeks, and the blue eyes were hidden in sleep.

CHAPTER VII.

LITTLE MARY'S LAST VISIT.

Some of the Archers' wealthy acquaintances, and notably Mr. Archer's sister, who had recently returned to town with her daughters, were greatly shocked when they chanced to hear of Pauline's fancy for little Mary Kelly.

"Of course I understand," said his sister, "that dear Ada is so much of an invalid that your poor child is left very much to the care of nurses and must contract odd ways. But are you not very imprudent, Reginald, to permit such an intimacy? In the first place, one never knows what infectious diseases children of that sort may bring about the house."

"The young cobbler," said Reginald, laughing, "is as sturdy as a colt so far. She looks much stronger than Pauline."

"But that apart," continued the worldly-wise matron, "isn't it a little dreadful to have Pauline playing with creatures out of a cellar? Really it is hard to tell what they may be like in any way."

"Oh, she's a mere infant, and well behaved they tell me," said Reginald.

"It might be even an undesirable connection hereafter," added the mentor, "when Pauline is grown up and going out. What if the girl were to presume on this childish friendship?"

Reginald Archer laughed outright. The idea of poor little Mary advancing any such claim appealed to his keen sense of humor. He had mentioned the circumstance to his sister as a curious, childish freak on Pauline's part, and his wife's relatives had been both amused and interested when they heard of it. So that, despite his laughter, he was rather annoyed, and his tone had a note of sharpness in it as he said:

"How absurd, Lulu! You fashionable women are too ridiculous, always taking fright at shadows. Why, later on, I intend to take Pauline abroad, and this little waif will disappear out of her life more completely than the pigeon they feed together."

He was a truer prophet than he knew at the time. His sister, silent but unconvinced, tapped with the pointed toe of her Parisian slipper as Reginald continued to defend his

Little Mary's Last Visit.   69

course, but not upon the higher grounds which his more refined wife would have taken.

"Why, think how many interests come into every child's life and pass out again; and our little one has been rather lonely. In fact, her mother was getting a bit anxious about her, and I think she was glad when she took so amazingly to this little mite."

"Does her mother know?" asked his sister. "Oh, then, of course there's no more to be said."

He quite understood the peculiar intonation and the even more expressive changing of the subject immediately, and it vexed him unreasonably. There had never been any sympathy between the sisters-in-law. Mrs. Archer's unvarying courtesy and gentleness had never warmed into cordiality with the brisk, somewhat bustling matron, who had but one thought—how best to advance herself and her daughters in the world. Their standards were different, their aims very far apart, and Reginald's sister regarded her brother's wife as somewhat peculiar and far too unworldly.

"Ada's a sweet creature," she used to say to her intimates, "but she cares nothing at all for society. I do think on Reginald's account

she ought to make more effort than she does.
I'm sure he regrets it, for he is of such a
social nature, though he's the soul of loyalty
and wouldn't find fault with his wife for the
world."

When Ada's chronic ill health had made
social life an impossibility, her sister-in-law
bewailed the husband's fate still more frequently.
So, although his sister pursued the
subject no farther, Reginald could read her
thoughts. He even understood the motive
which prompted his sister presently to say:

"You must bring Pauline here very often
now. Her cousins will enjoy having her, and
I'm sure it will be a treat to the child. She
has been, as you say, so much alone and is
liable to grow up peculiar. Besides, it will
be a preparation for later on. She will make
suitable acquaintances and acquire something
of a society manner. Poor Ada's health will
put her at such a disadvantage, and it has
kept you both out of everything these last
years."

Engrossed as Reginald Archer was with the
things that make for material prosperity, his
perceptions were not so much blunted that he
could desire formation for his little Pauline

after the model of those two very advanced young ladies, his nieces. They were sitting in the cushioned recesses of the window at the moment, carrying on a very spirited conversation with a young male visitor. Their discourse, which was pitched in a somewhat high key, was interrupted by peals of laughter, or by a variety of exclamations and a profusion of epithets. Everything was in a superlative degree. They never laughed, according to their own account of things, but shrieked or howled; they never cried, but bawled.

"No," thought Reginald Archer to himself with some bitterness, "the cobbler's child is preferable as a companion. Her influence would be negative, this other positive."

When he rose to take his leave he remarked that the doctor promised, if Ada kept as well as she then was, to let them go South for the winter.

"Have you decided where?" his sister asked.

"Either Florida or Bermuda," he answered.

"Either will be delightful. But you must really come as often as possible, and bring

Pauline with you. We don't see half enough of each other."

She was really fond of her brother, this ambitious society woman, and his wife had come of an extremely good family, so that they were very desirable connections.

"I will bring Pauline over some day soon to luncheon," he said; "it will be a change for her."

"Any time you like. We are nearly always here at luncheon about this season of the year."

Reginald exchanged a few words with his nieces, who effusively echoed their mother's invitation. He walked home in a very dissatisfied mood. His sister had made him feel that he was very hardly treated by fortune. She had, as it were, catalogued his grievances. His wife ill, his child neglected, and he himself kept out of congenial society by untoward events. There was no one to blame, and that rather added to his annoyance. He could not complain of Ada. She had been the best of wives, and he dared not disturb the enforced quiet of the sick-room by any allusion to his woes. Nor could he find fault with Pauline. So that, having no confidant and no scapegoat, his ill humor grew with every step he took in the homeward direction.

As he approached his own house he saw that Pauline, quite unconscious of his displeasure, sat upon the steps, playing at dolls with little Mary Kelly. His brow darkened, and passing the two children without a word, he entered the house, shutting the door with a bang. He threw his gloves upon the library table impatiently, and hung up his hat with the air of a martyr. After which he rang the bell for Rebecca, and ordered her to bring Pauline in and send the other child home.

"It's much too late in the afternoon for Miss Pauline to be out," he said irritably. "I wonder you don't look after her a little more."

"I'm to tell the child that's with her to go home," said Rebecca, overlooking the rebuke for the moment, and secretly glad of an opportunity to gratify her dislike of the cobbler's daughter. With the quickness of her class she caught some inkling of what was in her master's mind, and said impressively:

"I didn't never think, Mr. Archer, that it was just the right thing to have that little one coming here, but Miss Pauline she wanted her and—"

"Never mind that now," said Reginald, waving his hand impatiently, "it's time for the child to go home and for Miss Pauline to come in. That's all."

Rebecca, huffed at his manner and disappointed that he had declined to discuss the subject with her, opened the door and went out to the children. She revenged herself for her late snubbing by an additional accent of severity in her voice as she addressed the innocent object of her dislike. Her face at the moment, too, was so cross and forbidding in expression that little Mary felt inclined to cry as soon as she looked at her.

"You take your hat and go home," she said to the little girl. "You ought to have been gone home long ago, instead of being under Mr. Archer's feet when he got home."

"She wasn't under his feet," said the truthful Pauline; "she was away over here, and I don't think papa even noticed she was there."

"Didn't he, though!" said Rebecca with malicious triumph, "and he ringing the bell till I thought he was going to break it. What for, do you think?"

"I don't know," said Pauline.

"To get me to send her home."

Pauline's face grew crimson to the roots of her hair. She felt the slight to her playmate as though it had been to herself, but she could not think of a word to say. Little Mary looked from one to the other, not fully understanding what was said. But, frightened by Rebecca's looks, she began to put on her hat.

"Yes, you go straightway home," added Rebecca.

"How can you be so rude?" said Pauline, suddenly turning upon her nurse, with a stamp of her little foot. "Mary's going now, and if you don't let her alone I'll tell mamma."

Rebecca well knew that nothing would have more seriously displeased her mistress than what she had just done. Besides, the flash in Pauline's eyes told her that she must not go too far.

"You'd better talk to your papa about it," she said, turning to go in. "See what he says."

Poor little Mary's lip trembled and she began to cry. They had been interrupted in a glorious game of dolls by this cross woman who had told her to go away. She let her head hang down, as was her habit, till her hair, falling over her face, hid her tears, as she began slowly to descend the steps, carrying her own poor paintless doll with her. Pauline took her hand and walked down beside her to the foot of the steps.

"Don't cry, Mary," she said gently. "Sometimes Rebecca is cross to me, but I don't mind."

Pauline, but for her father's command to come into the house, would have walked part of the way with her disconsolate friend. But she watched the tiny figure making its way slowly down the street in its shabby dress, pausing every once in a while to wipe its eyes with its pinafore. Once the tear-stained face was turned backwards, as little Mary stood still to look at her friend standing in the light of the setting sun.

"You must come to-morrow, surely," called out Pauline.

The child smiled through her tears and walked on.

Little Mary did not come next day. In fact, her tiny feet never came up that street again. You may rest in peace, you over-respectable nurse and you irritable father. The cobbler's child will trouble you no more.

But Pauline, for the first time in her short life, stood before her father fearlessly and made complaint of her nurse.

"She was cruel to little Mary and made her cry," she began, "and she said that you told her to do it, and I don't believe it."

"I said something about it being too late for either of you to be out," Mr. Archer said uneasily.

There was something which abashed him in the flash of the blue eyes, usually so gentle, in the indignation which blazed out of the ordinarily quiet face. The affront which had been put upon her playmate and in her company had evidently wounded her to the heart. He regretted his hasty action, the more so that he felt the child was right and that the humblest guest should be treated with courtesy. But her resentment against Rebecca was not easily soothed.

"If she had told her politely that you said it was rather late to be out," said Pauline. And Reginald Archer, as a result of this conversation, was quite convinced that there were depths in the child's nature which he, at least, could not sound.

CHAPTER VIII.

WHY LITTLE MARY DID NOT COME.

WHEN two or three days had passed and little Mary did not appear, Mrs. Archer requested Rebecca to go and inquire what was the reason. Pauline had not said much to her mother of the unpleasant nature of the child's last visit, for she never liked to tell her anything which might disturb her. But she had said enough to make Mrs. Archer fancy that the little one had been hurt or wounded in some way, so that she did not wish to come any more, or else that the cobbler, hearing of it, had forbidden Mary to repeat her visits.

Pauline was privately of the same opinion, and she begged that she might be allowed to accompany Rebecca, and she herself speak to Mary.

Rebecca, who felt somewhat guilty with her mistress's clear gaze fixed upon her face, undertook the task, nevertheless with reluctance. She regarded little Mary's non-appearance in the light of a good riddance.

As they reached the head of the cellar steps, Rebecca going first, Pauline remarked how still it seemed to be below. There were no sounds of tacking or stitching, nor of little Mary talking at her play. Scarcely had Rebecca gone down two or three steps when the cobbler came out of the darkness. Catching sight of Pauline, he cried out hoarsely:

"For God's sake take her away! Don't let *her* come here, whatever you do."

Pauline stood still on the upper step, terrified. Why should the cobbler cry out to her to go away? She had always tried to be kind to little Mary, and had invented many little pleasures for her. Even if Mary had told him what Rebecca had said, surely she was not to blame. Her eyes filled with tears. But the next words explained:

"My little Mary has the fever, and the doctor says she may not live through the night."

With something between a sigh and a groan the cobbler disappeared into the darkness, whence his haggard face had emerged for an instant.

Pauline, still standing and looking after him, heard, as Rebecca came up to hurry her away, a faint, childish voice saying:

"Oh, daddy, it's the little lady. So bright! Is she a fairy, daddy?"

In after years Pauline sometimes thought that she might have imagined this, that it was but the echo of the words that had been spoken on her first visit to the cobbler's abode. But now she walked home awe-stricken by what she had heard, the nurse anxious and flurried—to do her justice, more on account of her charge than of herself. She was deeply shocked, moreover, for death is as awful in a cellar as in a palace, and her conscience smote her for her late unkindness to the little creature who was so soon to pass away from all their lives.

Pauline was awe-stricken, but not, as yet, deeply grieved. It is difficult for a child to realize what death is, or to believe that it can possibly come to one she holds dear. Far-reaching as the little girl's thoughts often were, she could not picture little Mary cold and still, as she had once seen a canary-bird. That incident had been long remembered, and gave her even yet a thrill of pain when it re-

Why Little Mary Did Not Come. 81

curred to her mind. Grave as she looked walking by Rebecca's side, she had almost persuaded herself, by the time they reached the door, that little Mary would soon be well again and coming to play with her.

Mrs. Archer caused fruit and jellies and other delicacies to be sent down, and even the careless Reginald, smitten like Rebecca with remorse, sent privately to offer the shoemaker some financial assistance if it became necessary. One day, when some delicacies had been sent, a message was returned that little Mary no longer needed them.

"Then she will be able to play with me soon," said Pauline, not understanding the nature of the communication.

"No, dear, little Mary will not be coming to play with you any more," said Mrs. Archer.

"Why, mamma?" asked Pauline, thinking vaguely of her father's displeased expression and her nurse's curt dismissal of her playmate.

"Because God has taken her to Himself," said Mrs. Archer.

Pauline's sensitive nature was completely overcome for the moment. She had grown to feel a real affection for her small playfellow, and remembered now the little figure and the sad, tear-stained face turned towards her for the last time, with an intensity of grief which alarmed her mother.

"Pauline, my dearest Pauline," she said, "doesn't God know best? He has taken little Mary from a cellar to His own bright kingdom."

The attendant, fearing the result of the child's agitation on her mother, caused her to withdraw, and Mrs. Archer, left alone, pondered deeply on the mystery of suffering which this life can never solve. She thought of the childless father in the gloom of his now solitary cellar, and the budding existence cut short, while her own was spinning itself wearily along. But she seemed later to realize more fully the depth of the poor cobbler's grief from the description which Pauline gave of him. He appeared to have given up his work, and spent much of his time walking up and down on the far side of the street, looking always towards their house, where his little Mary had had so many happy hours.

"He looks very old," Pauline said to her mother, "and all gathered up together. And there are places in his face, as if he was always crying."

Mrs. Archer thought within herself that it would have given her real pleasure to have been able to go out and speak a few words of sympathy and hope to the forlorn cobbler. But it was impossible.

One day, as he passed, Pauline was sitting on the top step, with her doll and the pigeon beside her, just as Mary had described. He fled from the sight, a swift pang convulsing his rugged features and a sob rising to his lips. But the second time he saw her he stood still, staring at the little girl with a wistful intensity. With a sudden impulse Pauline arose and crossed the street. She did not know very well what to say, but her first words took the form of a wish.

"Oh, I wish little Mary was back," she said earnestly, the tears gathering in her eyes.

"Don't wish that," said the cobbler in a hoarse voice which somehow did not startle Pauline. "Whatever you wish, don't wish that. Wish that my heart would stop aching and break at once, but don't ask her back."

Pauline's blue eyes gazed wonderingly at him, but she intuitively felt the agony which was wringing his strong frame, and the tears, overflowing, fell down her cheeks unchecked on to her frock.

"God bless you, little miss! From my heart I say it," said the man, trying to speak less roughly. "You gave her 'most all the pleasure she ever had. I did what I could, but, O God, she lived and died under the street, in a cellar!"

"But she went to heaven just as quick," said Pauline. "God doesn't care where people live."

"It's the only hope we poor have," the man said. "If it weren't for that, how could we live at all, at all? But I'll not keep you, missy," he went on after a pause. "I'm no company for the likes of you, and mebbe they'll be wanting you at home, as I'm wanting my little Mary—and she'll never come." He turned away with the same sharp agony, so like despair.

"I want to tell you," said Pauline, "my mother's sorry, sorry. If she only could come out, she would tell you so. But she can't; she's always ill."

"May God spare her to you!" said the man, "for it was a good mother gave you the heart you have. And she was kind, kind in our sore trouble. Tell her from me that there's one blessing will follow her day and night, and that's mine. And now I'll go. I'm too long here as it is."

"Good-by," said Pauline, holding out her hand.

He took it, and wrung it hard in his own rough hand, upon which one of the little girl's tears fell and glistened like a pearl. He went slowly and wistfully away after that, as one who does not very well know where he is going or what he means to do.

Pauline went home, saying not a word to her nurse, but waiting till she had an opportunity of telling her mother.

"I wanted to tell him to pray to Holy Mary, because that would make him feel better," she said, "but I was ashamed; and I think he does anyway, because he taught Mary her prayers, and she knew them very well."

"Poor man! poor heart-broken man!" said Mrs. Archer, and she pictured to herself the rough shoemaker teaching the tiny creature her prayers in the darkness of the cellar. But sympathetic as Mrs. Archer was, she could not guess at half the pathos of the simple life-story so tragically ended: the poor man's anxious contrivings to procure for his little one proper food, whatever he might have himself; his efforts to keep her from the rude jarring of life, or from evil, and to brighten the cheerlessness of their existence by giving her glimpses of the fairy world of the imagination, which had come to him as an inheritance from the green land over the waters. After Pauline had come as a ray of sunshine across little Mary's path, the cobbler's endeavors to make her decent before she went up to play at the big house were full of pathos. He anxiously sorted over the little frocks, and put a stitch here and a patch there. He combed and even curled the child's hair and saw that her hands and face were clean. All this had been a labor of love to him, and her outings made him almost as happy as they had Mary. He knew that she was safe and well cared for when she was in Pauline's company, and though he missed her at odd times, still he sang or whistled at his work, stitching and tacking energetically all the time she was away, and looking forward to her return. When it was near time he would begin to listen, till at last he heard the busy little feet pattering on the pavement and descending the steps, while the childish lips were fairly overflowing with the tale she had to tell. He had actually saved enough to get her a new dress and a hat in case Pauline's father should ever take Mary out with them again. For the passing freak of a good-natured, rich man had been an event in these two simple lives. The dress was now hung up unworn, and the hat had been thrust out of the desolate father's sight with a groan. Faith alone saved his reason in that hour of darkness.

When Pauline repeated the cobbler's message to her mother, the latter said:

" The prayers of the poor are very precious. That blessing he has promised me will be as a rich inheritance."

CHAPTER IX.

PAULINE GOES VISITING.

PAULINE often wet the pigeon's shimmering plumage with her tears, as she sat alone on the steps and told him over and over the story of little Mary's death.

"She is fretting for her little playmate," Mrs. Archer said to her husband, "and on such a nature as hers the occurrence may have a serious effect."

"Do you find her looking ill?" cried Reginald with sudden alarm. The tragedy of Mary's death had brought the possibilities home to him, and he felt a chill at his heart at thought of anything happening to Pauline. Perhaps she had caught that terrible fever!

"Oh, no," said Mrs. Archer, laying a soothing hand on his arm. "She is grieving somewhat, that is all. So I will be glad when the time comes for her to have a change."

"I promised Lulu, by the way, to bring her over there to luncheon some day soon."

"That will be very nice indeed for her," said Mrs. Archer.

"I think I shall take her over there this afternoon," said Reginald, who liked to act on impulse, "and then we can arrange what day next week she may go to luncheon."

"Very well," said Mrs. Archer. "Rebecca will have her ready about four o'clock, I suppose."

"Yes, somewhere about that time. And now I must be off."

On their way to his sister's Reginald Archer, brisk, alert, and good-natured as usual, pointed out to Pauline the various public buildings, club-houses, private dwellings, or churches, with that peculiar pride felt by a genuine New-Yorker in the brick-and-mortar glories of his splendid city.

Pauline looked indifferently at the great stone mansions which had been familiar to her since childhood, but she was far more interested in the churches. Their vast proportions seemed especially to appeal to her, and every once in a while she asked her father:

"Papa, is that a Catholic church?" It was always with a feeling of disappointment that she heard that this or that noble pile was a Presbyterian or a Baptist or a Congregational church.

"It must have been nice when every church was Catholic," said Pauline.

"That was never the case in New York."

"Oh, I mean in all the world, in the old times," cried Pauline, after which she relapsed into silence, amusing herself by naming every church which they passed.

"That one might be the Sacred Heart, and that Holy Mary's Church, and that St. Joseph's, and this tiny one St. John's."

Instead she read upon some of them the names.

"Just of people," she said, and her little mind was filled with a great desire to rechristen them all after the glorious company of martyrs or the heroic host of confessors and apostles. She took a variety of notes on other subjects as she went along. How the horses' feet tripped over the rough cobblestones or macadamized pavement to a rhythmic measure, and the people paced the sidewalks with the air of taking part in a show. She noted the florists' windows, wherein the late flowers made splendid patches of color, red, yellow, or purple, with green and white softening them to the eyes; and the caterers' shops decorated with bonbonnières in fascinating variety, alternated with dainty piles of delicious sweets or cakes, with icings multicolored and dreamlike in delicacy.

The visit to her aunt's was a great success, though the head of the house was absent. But the two gushing young cousins were at home, and entertained their relatives very prettily at afternoon tea.

"She's sweet," said one of these youthful enthusiasts to Reginald, indicating Pauline, who sat erect on one of the Louis XV. chairs, behaving with her usual decorum and propriety.

"A perfect dear," said the other, who was something of an artist and went in for being æsthetic. "Why, Uncle Reginald, she's a poem, a symphony in flesh and blood."

Pauline caught the word, and treasured it for future use. She could not imagine why this Cousin Mollie made her sit in different chairs and put her head against various-colored curtains, with light falling on her from more than one point.

"She has the most exquisite eyes," added Mollie, "and her hair is a dream."

Reginald was not at all displeased by these raptures, and left the house in high good humor, having promised to bring Pauline to luncheon on a certain appointed day.

"Do come early," cried the girls, who, in their own way, were good-natured and sociable. "There are heaps of things about the house we want to show Pauline."

The latter had observed with her calm blue eyes the various details of the elaborately furnished house, the great drawing-rooms, the conservatory, and the Parisian costumes of her cousins, but always with the reserve and perfect breeding which were habitual to her.

"What's a symphony?" she asked her mother that evening. Pauline pronounced the word imperfectly, so that at first her mother could not catch it, nor did she find it easy to make the meaning clear to her little daughter.

"Why do you want to know?" she asked.

"Cousin Mollie said I was that," said Pauline. "Of course I didn't know what she meant."

"She meant it kindly, dear," said her mother, "but I don't think you could quite understand its meaning."

Pauline asked no more, but she repeated the word often to herself, and it was uncomfortably associated in her mind for a long time after with Cousin Mollie.

"I wonder what it is," she said to herself. "It sounds queer, but I'll know when I'm big."

After that Pauline's attention was altogether taken up with preparations for the departure to the South, a probable date having been decided on. Her wardrobe had to be overlooked, additions made to it, old frocks ripped up and turned, hats retrimmed or renewed. In fact there was a great deal to be done.

Mrs. Archer was so much better that the doctor thought the journey would be quite safe, and that it should be made before the mild weather was quite over. Reginald Archer was not only delighted with the improvement in his wife's health, but he was glad of a change. So that the bustle in the household during those autumn days was altogether a pleasant one. Even Rebecca thawed in advance, as though the genial sun of the South had already touched her. She, as well as Mrs. Archer's personal attendant, was to accompany them. For Reginald Archer's speculations had been very fortunate of late, and he laughingly assured his wife that she need not be one bit anxious about the expense. Pauline, in the nursery, thinking over all the new things that were being got and of what she had heard would be the cost of the journey, exclaimed once to Rebecca:

"We aren't poor at all."

A sudden memory struck her of how she had once said the very same thing and had added:

"But little Mary Kelly is."

She did not utter the thought aloud this time. She had never mentioned Mary's name to Rebecca since the day when the child had been sent home. But like a shadow the tiny child flitted across her mind; a shadow soon to grow dim in the excitement of new scenes, but never entirely to fade away.

As she stood looking out of the window, her eyes striving to pierce the radiant sunset, she wondered in what bright place Mary was now.

"She isn't poor any more," she said to herself with awe. "Little Mary's rich and very beautiful."

She pictured her playfellow as she had seen saints in pictures, with a shining robe and something like the sun behind her head. And

watching the golden mist which floated over
the sky, she wondered if that were what
heaven was like.

"If she had to come back to the cellar
now!" she thought.

But here her meditations were interrupted
by Mademoiselle Nouvelle, who had come to
try on her new frock. The dressmaker was
full of smiles and compliments as she adjusted
every plait and frill.

"I wonder if I look like a symphony now,"
thought Pauline with a funny little laugh, instantly suppressed. In fact she was very
grave, and submitted to be turned and twisted
in all directions. Only her blue eyes looked
curiously at the volatile Frenchwoman. Pauline often had a variety of thoughts about
people, but she was happily far too polite to
express them. She wondered now why
Mademoiselle's head kept bobbing up and
down, and how all the hair she had stayed in
its place.

"Perhaps it's the same kind as Rebecca's,"
she reflected, "and then she can take it off at
night."

She rather envied Rebecca that privilege
when she used to watch her put her hair on

a chair to brush it. For one of Pauline's minor trials had been the vigorous process to which her own tresses were subjected at the hands of Rebecca. She also thought Rebecca was fortunate in having teeth which came out. "I can't take out any of mine," the child often said. "I wish I could."

The Frenchwoman was of course quite unconscious of Pauline's thoughts, and continued to address her in voluble and somewhat jerky sentences.

"Your robe fits you to a marvel," she said.

It seemed funny to Pauline that her frock should be called a robe, but she gave no sign.

"And your figure, it is a perfection."

Pauline gave the woman an inscrutable look as she continued:

"You are straight as the darts. Oh, how it is a pleasure to make the robes for you!"

The frock was a very pretty one, and the dressmaker more skilful with the needle than in the use of the English language.

"I am not large in the English speech," she observed. "I cannot much speak."

Pauline thought she managed to speak a good deal, but her attention was diverted by the rows of pretty buttons and the artistic bows of ribbon. She was delighted with her new dress.

"The color goes so well for you," said Mademoiselle. "It brings out the tint of your cheek, which resembles to the rose."

Pauline was quite unused to flattery, with the exception of the few gushing remarks, but half understood, of her cousins. Rebecca had sternly set her face against anything of the kind from the first, and Mrs. Archer had purposely avoided it. So that it did not appeal to Pauline; nor did she because of it feel any attraction towards those who used it.

To do the Frenchwoman justice, she had not set herself deliberately to flatter her little customer. She sincerely admired the child. The graceful, slender figure and upright carriage appealed to her professional instincts, while the blue eyes and shining hair pleased the artistic feeling common to people of her race. She took as much trouble as possible in fitting and finishing the dainty costume, which was to be one of Pauline's best. Mrs. Archer had always insisted upon the most perfect simplicity in her little daughter's dress, and in this her views agreed with the Frenchwoman's ideas of what was proper for a child.

CHAPTER X.

PAULINE'S COUSINS.

It was in this very costume that Pauline stood prepared to accompany her father to luncheon at Aunt Lulu's. She went out upon the sidewalk and began to pace slowly up and down in the sunshine, while her father was dressing with unusual care. He was going to a very fashionable reception later in the day. As Pauline walked, observing the sunbeams, and wondering how they managed to make their way in and out of the grayness of the pavement, and to fleck the dust of the road without really touching it, she suddenly heard the familiar voices of her former persecutors, the street-boys. Whether it was that their own particular neighborhood had furnished them with some new attraction, or for whatever reason, they had not lately troubled the little girl. Perceiving her now, they cried out in glee:

"Oh, there's Miss Proudie! She's still alive, and more stuck up than ever."

"I say," cried one, "are you any relation to Queen Victory?"

"Her daughter, mebbe," cried another; "the Princess Victory."

"Gosh! ain't she fine in her new rig!"

Pauline cast one of her inscrutable looks towards them as she walked up the steps very slowly, lest they might think she was running away, and stood still there, facing them.

"Miss Proudie's got it bad this morning," cried one of the-gang. "Her nose is goin' up so high it won't come down no more. Take care you don't lose it, sissy."

These exclamations were accompanied by yells which resembled nothing so much as an Indian war-whoop. This musical entertainment was cut short by the sudden opening of the door, and the appearance of Reginald Archer.

"Cricky! there's her dad!" cried the chorus. "My eyes! what a swell! Look out for squalls when she tells him."

So saying, every head disappeared in a jiffy into a neighboring area. But Pauline disdained to make any complaint of them.

"They're only street-boys," she said to herself, "and don't know any better."

But when she was driving away in the hansom which her father had called, with the crisp air blowing in her face and touching it into color, she continued the subject in her own mind.

"I wonder if they always live in the street," she thought, "or if they ever go into houses."

The term street-boys, which she had first heard from Rebecca, conveyed a rather vague impression to her mind. Her father was of course quite unconscious of her thoughts, and he was himself rather silent, being occupied with some matter of business.

Pauline's aunt unconsciously echoed the very sentiment of the street-boys, though it would have filled her aristocratic soul with horror to have been told that she could have anything in common with such creatures.

"Why, Reginald, she's a perfect little princess," she said; and her brother was the more pleased by this half-involuntary tribute of admiration because he knew that his sister was not given to lavishing praises on any but her own girls.

Aunt Lulu, having thus pronounced upon her niece, began to converse upon some topic of common interest to her brother and herself, and Pauline was whirled away by her cousins to amuse and be amused until luncheon. They found the little girl's quaint notions, as far as her shyness permitted her to express them, simply fascinating. They took her to what had been the nurseries, but which to these early-emancipated young ladies of fifteen and sixteen were but a distant memory.

"Ever so long ago we used to have our meals in here," they said, throwing open the door of a small square apartment which had once been used as a dining-room. The day-nursery was full of juvenile treasures, such as simple Pauline had never imagined. She had had her own share of toys, and even at times costly ones, but this collection was bewildering. Dolls with complete trousseaux, including everything in mimic counterfeit that even the most modern young lady could possess, with trunks of the newest patterns, bedsteads, folding and otherwise, wardrobes and bureaus and secretaries with endless shelves and drawers. There was furniture of every kind: sofas, armchairs, dining-tables set out with every appliance, rocking-chairs and footstools. There were tea-sets and bedroom-sets, and dinner-sets in china and pewter, with baby-houses and kitchens which had more dishes and cooking-utensils than even the modern grown-up kitchens. There were books of exquisite design and coloring which made Pauline open her eyes wide in delight. And then the mechanical toys: walking dolls and talking dolls and sleeping dolls; lambs that bleated, donkeys that brayed, carriages that drove swiftly over the nursery floor, figures that moved their hands, employed in a variety of trades; trains that started on mimic journeys, express-carts that rattled almost as much as the big ones. There were other great carts laden with bags and boxes and barrels, and Pauline took delight in unloading these at the doors of grocery-shops with the dearest little cannisters and a real till, through which money which looked real could be slipped.

Pauline was still young enough to love toys, so she fairly revelled in this toy-kingdom, where the Santa Claus she had once believed in could easily have filled his pack.

"How did you ever get so many?" she asked of her cousins.

"Oh, and we broke lots more," said they carelessly, "and gave away heaps."

"Little Mary Kelly would have been just sure this was fairyland," Pauline said involuntarily; for since her playmate's death she had not mentioned her name, except to her mother.

"Mary Kelly?" echoed the cousins.

"She was a little girl I used to know," said Pauline. "She's dead now."

"Oh!" said the listeners.

"She was very poor, I think," said Pauline, "and once when we took her to the Park she thought it was fairyland."

Cousin Mollie suddenly began to remember the story of Pauline's odd fancy for some low child, and she asked:

"How did a child of that sort know anything about fairies?"

She spoke as if the fairy world in some sort belonged to the children of the rich and was not to be approached by less favored ones.

"She knew very well," said Pauline. "Her father told her."

"But wasn't she a cobbler's child?" asked the younger cousin, who also remembered suddenly. "How could a poor man who was always busy mending shoes have time to talk about fairies ? "

" I don't know," said Pauline in her slow, deliberate speech. " Perhaps he wasn't always mending shoes, so sometimes he could talk about fairies."

" But where did he ever hear of them ? " cried both the cousins, seeming to be quite aggrieved at his knowledge.

Pauline could not explain this difficulty.

" It must have just come into his head," she said; " people think of such lots of things— unless some one told him. But if little Mary could have seen all these ! She just had one tiny doll, with the paint off one side of its face, and no clothes for it. She brought it up to our house sometimes, and once I made a dress and a petticoat for it, and little Mary ran home to tell her father about it, she was so glad. She wouldn't even wait till I made a waist."

The cousins were silent. Perhaps a sudden thought occurred to them, in the mass of superfluities by which they were surrounded, of lives, like this one just gone out, which have had so little in them.

" She was a very nice little girl," said Pauline, "and just big enough to get up the cellar stairs alone and come up about two blocks to our house."

The mention of the cellar jarred upon the listeners. It seemed dreadful to have any one coming from such a place into one's house.

"I thought it awful to have to live in a cellar at first," said Pauline, "and that's why I wanted her to come up pretty often; and so did mamma when she found she was a nice little girl. But," she added, warming to her theme and sitting back on the floor, surrounded by a confusion of packages which she had just unloaded from the express-cart, "it doesn't make any difference now. Isn't it strange to think that little Mary has more than all this?"

She waved her hands to indicate the nursery with all its treasures.

"And more than all the city full of things," she added impressively.

Her two cousins sat still in the armchairs into which they had thrown themselves, regarding the little girl before them with curiosity. It must be owned, too, that they were somewhat impressed by the idea thus presented to them in the imperfect speech of childhood.

"After she was dead," Pauline continued in a hushed voice, "her father looked as if he was nearly always crying. He wasn't crying when I saw him, but he said that he wished his heart would stop aching and break at once."

Perhaps it was a revelation to the spoiled darlings of fortune who listened that a cobbler had a heart, much more one that was liable to break. If they had thought of the matter at all, they would have concluded that people of that sort, to use their own vague expression, couldn't feel anything very keenly.

"It was awful to see him," said Pauline; "and I think I would have been afraid of him when he spoke in a queer voice, only that I knew he was just feeling sorry for little Mary and couldn't help speaking like that. Sometimes I speak queerly when I'm sorry about anything. Perhaps he feels better now, though."

Pauline concluded her speech with this comforting thought, and went briskly back to the loading of the express-cart, making the donkey's head wag, too, while she stuffed various small bundles into the panniers at each side of him.

"I think I'll play I'm a robber, soon," she said, adding politely, "that is, if you don't mind. I'll be coming on that horse over there to stop a train of provisions."

But her cousins being quite willing, those somewhat bored young ladies being very much amused by her vagaries, she had assumed a dozen different disguises before luncheon.

"You're so original, dear," said Cousin Mollie.

"What's that?" asked Pauline, stopping in the act of doing sentry duty before a fort she had erected out of blocks.

"Oh, I don't know, but it's charming."

Pauline resumed her sentry-work. She had been afraid for the moment that she might have been making herself disagreeable to her cousins.

Luncheon being presently announced, she accompanied her cousins down-stairs.

CHAPTER XI.

A LUNCHEON AT AUNT LULU'S.

As Pauline seated herself at the luncheon-table, Reginald Archer could not help casting a swift glance of pride at her. Her cheeks were flushed a little and her eyes bright from her recent experiences in the kingdom of toys up-stairs.

"Have you had a pleasant hour with your cousins up-stairs?" asked Pauline's aunt in her conventional voice.

"Yes, thank you, Aunt Lulu," responded Pauline in a subdued tone. Her shyness, which had worn off a good deal with her cousins, returned in the presence of her somewhat formal aunt. Pauline did not permit herself any reflections disparaging to this lady, whose face, with its artificial smiles and forced kindliness, was still almost an exact copy of her father's.

"Did you take her to the nursery, girls?" asked Aunt Lulu.

"Oh, yes, mamma, and she was so sweet, playing with the toys."

Pauline, demurely eating her luncheon off the most exquisite of hand-painted china, peeped from behind the Venetian bowl of late roses which hid her view, to see what her aunt might think of this complimentary reference to herself. But that lady had quite forgotten the matter, and as she took her iced bouillon from the silver cup she confided to her brother a new scheme which she had in view for the girls.

"I think it will be charming, and several of our friends have taken it up for their daughters. If Pauline were a few years older, she might have joined the band. They will sail in January, and travel abroad for a year or so."

"But haven't they been over half a dozen times?" asked practical Reginald, leaning back in his chair to wait for the substantials.

"Only three times," corrected his sister.

"But hasn't Mollie seen almost everything over there?"

"This is *such* a chance, though," said his sister. "A delightful lot of girls going, and with such an experienced person. They are to have regular hours for study, and in doing the art-galleries and places of note are to learn everything about them."

"How will you girls take to all that study?" asked Uncle Reginald. "What do you say, Mollie?"

Mollie made an expressive little gesture to signify that she was not likely to study too much, but she said aloud:

"Of course we'll study. We have to be up in all sorts of things; but that won't prevent us from having an uproarious time. We're sure to enjoy ourselves."

"Why, certainly, my love," said her mother, "enjoyment is the great business of life at your age. Pauline, you shall have your turn at it, later."

Reginald Archer was much too good-natured and indisposed to trouble himself about other people's concerns to argue the matter any further. But he mentally thought that he would never allow Pauline to go away with strange people and have "an uproarious time." The words seemed absurd in connection with that child, whose blue eyes, heavily fringed, looked on the world with an expression which her nurse called "creepy."

Luncheon over, Reginald declared that he had to take Pauline home before he went to a reception at the Union League Club. So Pauline was kissed and gushed over, with many injunctions from aunt and cousins alike to be sure and come again soon. Reginald told them that they hoped to get away very soon, but that later Pauline would see more of them.

Pauline took leave without much regret of the great drawing-rooms opening one into another, with vistas of exquisite ornaments, screens, and oriental palms growing, as it were, in this luxuriance of wealth. The dining-room, with its conservatory full of plants and flowers, was on the opposite side of the hall and was equally rich and beautiful.

Pauline had much to reflect upon, and there were various questions she wanted to ask her mother when she was admitted to the invalid's room about twilight. She told her, in the first place, about those wonderful toys and how she was rather afraid to touch them at first until her cousins had told her that she could do as she pleased with them, for that they didn't care for toys at all.

"But it would have been just awful to

break any, I would have been so ashamed," bringing her brows together expressively. "So I touched them all very gently and played carefully with them."

"That was the wisest thing to do," said the mother, knowing well that it is not always safe to take people at their word. "One should be always careful in handling other people's things."

"Were they ever children?" asked Pauline.

"Who, your cousins? Why, of course; they are little more than children now."

"Some people seem as if they had always been grown up," said Pauline, "and I think Cousin Mollie would look funny in a pinafore."

She began to laugh, thinking of her cousin's fashion-plate appearance with over-decorated hair.

"I'm almost sure she never skipped or ran, or played robbers or anything like that. She says she used to adore dolls ever so long ago."

Pauline's unconscious imitation of her cousin's speech made Mrs. Archer smile as she said:

"Mollie's just sixteen now."

"Is she?" said Pauline. "Aunt Lulu's quite young, too, isn't she?"

This unexpected question nearly upset the invalid's gravity.

"Comparatively young, yes," she said.

"Her cheeks are very fresh," said Pauline, "and she would look a good deal like papa if she had whiskers on."

"They are alike and yet different," said Mrs. Archer, waiting for Pauline's next question, which came presently.

"What's uproarious?" she asked.

"It usually means loud, noisy," said Mrs. Archer. "But how was it used?"

"Cousin Mollie said she would have an uproarious time when she went to Europe. I didn't know what she meant, because I don't think I ever heard that word before."

It struck Pauline's fancy, though, and she used it after that frequently in her plays.

"It sounds funny, very funny," she said to herself.

When she went down after a while to feed the pigeon, she said to it:

"If you could fly far as birds do, and go far, far away, over the roofs, you'd have an uproarious time."

The pigeon might have said that he could have flown much farther if his wings had not been clipped, but he said nothing, only picked up the crumbs, standing beside his little patron in the setting sun.

"I wish I could fly," she said to herself. "I'd just love to start from our chimney and go up high into the air. But I can't, and so I think I'll ask Rebecca to come up on the roof with me to fly a kite. It will be lovely to see it going away in the breeze."

She bade the pigeon good-by, as she had to go in to tea, which she generally took alone, for, except on state occasions, she never went to dinner with her father. Indeed, since his wife had been obliged to keep her room Mr. Archer often dined at the club.

"There will be only a few more teas and dinners before we start," Pauline said to Rebecca as the latter served the simple meal.

"I hope so," said Rebecca, who was rather vexed that the journey had been delayed longer than she expected.

"Are you going to wear your lily-of-the-valley dress the day we go?" asked Pauline, referring to a red calico with sprays of white which Rebecca had lately purchased.

"Oh, I suppose I'll have to make myself fine, or you'll be for leaving me behind," said the nurse with grim humor.

"No," said Pauline, "I'd rather you'd go, and I don't care how you dress."

"Anything'll do for me," said Rebecca caustically.

"I didn't mean that," said Pauline. "I like you in your lily-of-the-valley dress very much."

"Oh, well, anything's becoming to a beauty," said the nurse, "so I needn't be anxious."

"There's a tiny Japanese lady on this plate," said Pauline, changing the subject, "and she looks as if she was standing on a frog's head. No, it's a butterfly with speckled wings. He looks very big, but when I put down my piece of cake it covers him and the lady and that man with the big hat and the umbrella. I look as big, as big beside that lady as the elephant looked near little Mary and me."

A shadow fell over her face as she said these last words, and she finished her meal in silence, to Rebecca's satisfaction, as that worthy woman was hurrying to have a long evening out.

CHAPTER XII.

A JOURNEY.

WHEN the day of departure came at last, one of Pauline's chief regrets was to have to leave the pigeon. She felt sure he would not be there when she got back. The old cook, who was staying in the house with her niece, the housemaid, and with whom Pauline was a great favorite, promised to look after it. Having thus disposed of her worldly affairs, Pauline was the first to go out when the carriage came to the door to take them away. She caught a glimpse of some of her old enemies, the street-boys, but they were strangely silent, staring at the carriage with the valises upon it. It didn't matter now, Pauline thought, what they said or did.

Pauline, though she had been looking forward to the journey with a child's love of change, felt a sharp, homesick pang when the carriage door banged upon her father, her mother, and herself, and, the coachman mounting to his seat, they were driven away. She felt as if the house were some dearly loved friend from whom she was parting, and the cook, who stood waving to her from the area, some one whose real value she had never known before. The windows of her mother's room, with tightly closed shutters, and those of her own nursery looked so lonely as the carriage turned the corner, shutting the familiar block from sight.

"It seems strange that we won't be going back there to-night," she said to herself. "It will be all dark except the basement, and the nursery will be ghostly."

Her father, who was very much elated at the prospect of the journey, chatted away with her mother, who seemed wonderfully well, until they reached the wharf where the great steamer lay waiting to take them on board. They went at once to their state-rooms, the best on board, for which Mr. Archer had paid extra on his wife's account, and it cheered Pauline to see Rebecca's familiar figure bustling about among the luggage. She and Mrs. Archer's attendant had gone down beforehand, at the same time as the larger luggage, to see that all was properly placed.

Pauline presently went up with her father to the deck, where, amidst a pleasant, jostling crowd all saying good-by or giving farewell messages, Reginald discovered Aunt Lulu and the girls, who brought sweets for Pauline and flowers for Mrs. Archer. They had not much time to stay, and had barely gone when there was a creaking and a straining, and a blowing of signals, and finally a great swish of water, which told that they were off. Pauline's heart gave a great bound. It seemed strange to her to be sailing away from the one shore she had so far known, as she watched the gradual disappearance of church-spires and tall buildings and innumerable roofs, upon which fell the slanting afternoon sun, till at last all had vanished, as places vanish in a dream.

After that Pauline felt cross and miserable. She had one of what Rebecca called her bad turns.

"Though she ain't often cross," she remarked to Mrs. Archer's attendant afterwards, "but she has a temper, and I suppose it's better, or one might be thinkin' she was too good for this world."

Pauline was distinctly cross and troublesome. Her overstrained nerves reacted on her tired body, and she fought Rebecca outright and had to be put into the berth almost by force. She lay there sobbing out:

"Oh, you wretched, wretched Rebecca, I wish you were in—Africa!"

Rebecca reduced her to silence at length, saying by a happy inspiration that she was "keepin' her sick ma awake." This acted like a charm, and Pauline with wonderful self-control hushed her sobs, crying softly to herself, saying, however, as a last dart at Rebecca:

"I wish it was the last day, I'm so tired."

"Sakes alive!" muttered Rebecca, half scared by the wish, which out upon the face of the waters struck her as a tempting of Providence.

The weary little wanderer was very soon asleep. The rush of the water, and the other noises of the vessel as it ploughed through the waters like some mighty monster, which had at first frightened her, helped to lull her into slumber.

Next morning she was herself again, but she felt uncomfortab' and remorseful all day, though Rebecca had forgotten, or seemed to have forgotten, all about the previous night. To Mrs. Archer Pauline said:

"Children are a great deal worse than big people. I fought with Rebecca last night. I'm almost sure I pinched her, and I would have liked to kick her."

"A great girl like you!" said Mrs. Archer. "Oh, why did you behave in that way to poor Rebecca, when she was so tired and had so much to do?"

"I don't know," said Pauline gloomily. "I called her 'wretched Rebecca,' and said I wished she was in Africa."

"It was well for you that your foolish wish wasn't granted," said Mrs. Archer, trying to look serious. "You must tell your nurse that you're sorry, and try to be yourself the rest of the journey. You must have been overtired yourself, I think."

"Perhaps I was," said Pauline; and after a while she went to find Rebecca, who seemed very cross and was grumbling about the accommodations on shipboard.

"I'm sorry I was so cross last night," she

said, "and I don't wish you were in Africa at all, Rebecca."

"I couldn't be much worse than where I am," said the nurse grimly.

Pauline began to laugh.

"I was just thinking how funny you'd look in Africa, among the black, woolly people."

Rebecca looked at her sourly, but said nothing. She did not choose to imagine herself in any such situation.

"You might get speared," said Pauline, "just like that," seizing an umbrella to illustrate her meaning.

"Quit your foolishness," said the nurse, and Pauline ran gayly away. She was the only child on board, and was made a great pet of by the passengers and allowed many privileges by the captain. It was good to see her running with swift steps from deck to deck, with shining hair flying and cheeks glowing.

There was a Japanese on board, who took a great fancy to the little girl, and showed her many curios which he carried in a kind of hand-satchel. He had not packed them in a trunk, he told her, for fear they might get broken. He asked Pauline if she did not think a tiny idol which he had was beautiful. It was the great Buddha himself. Pauline was silent, and the truth-loving child told her mother afterwards:

"He was just hideous. I couldn't say he was pretty. His eyes were tight-closed, and he had earrings in his ears, and he was squatting down just like this."

Pauline's effort to show the attitude of the great Buddha caused a shout of laughter from her father, who had drawn near unperceived to the invalid's deck-chair, near which was Pauline. Pauline reddened. She was rather shy in her father's presence. The Japanese had shown her, too, the loveliest bits of china, and had explained to her some of the queer symbols upon them. He brought forth small objects in gold and silver which would have made an expert in such matters leap for joy, and handkerchiefs and scarfs of finest silk, and fans of fairy-like texture and workmanship. Pauline loved to look at all these things and to hear the man talk. He told her of the great chrysanthemum show in his country, and of the perfection to which these flowers are carried there:

"Because," said he, "they are the emblem of the Mikado, the Son of Heaven."

He described the temple of Buddha, Gate of the Eternal, and the tea-houses, and the shrines, which were a dream of loveliness, and the bazars and silk-shops, and the divine mountain rising out of the sea, and the country fragrant and glowing with pink-and-white cherry-blossoms.

"When I am big I would like to go there," said Pauline to her mother.

"Ah, my dear," said Mrs. Archer, with a half-melancholy smile, "who knows how far those little feet will have to carry you?"

Pauline's account of the Japanese collection inspired Rebecca with a great desire to see it. But the Japanese was inexorable. To Pauline and to Pauline alone would he show it.

"Perhaps he only likes to show them to children," said Pauline in explanation.

The two days on shipboard passed all too quickly. The sun grew warmer and warmer as the ship sped southward. Pauline loved to stand on the main deck, outside of the great saloon, and let the wind blow in and out of her hair, and the salt spray moisten her cheeks.

At last the green hills of the land they were approaching came in sight. Pauline's father called her to see the first sight of land, and the pilot approaching in a tiny boat.

"What is a pilot?" asked Pauline.

"A man that's got to bring us safe through the reefs," answered her father.

Mrs. Archer was also on deck in her steamer-chair comfortably arranged with cushions and rugs, so that together they all saw the water with its marvellous green color, so clear, as it nears the shore, that the coral reef is visible below.

"It looks like a great beach where it would be lovely to run," cried Pauline, "and it isn't so very far down."

"Oh, isn't it!" said her father. "The water here is more fathoms deep than you would care to count."

Pauline politely said good-by to the captain and the passengers, especially the Japanese, before leaving the ship. She was delighted to land on that lovely shore. They drove along a smooth, level road towards the hotel, and the child had her first glimpse of the wonderful tropical vegetation, the tall palms, the flowering shrubs, the rich bloom of the

South. A black man driving a long two-wheeled cart drawn by a donkey saluted them from under his wide-brimmed straw hat with a grin. His appearance made Pauline realize that she was really in a foreign land. At the hotel they had splendid rooms looking out over the harbor and far to seaward, and going down to supper Mr. Archer was as charmed with the flavor of the celebrated "angel-fish" as his daughter was with the almost magical fruits put before her. It all seemed like a page from the Arabian Nights, and Pauline was eager for the night to be over and another day to begin.

CHAPTER XIII.

REBECCA GETS A FRIGHT.

PAULINE had asked Rebecca to wake her very early next morning; but the little girl was really up first, and dressing hastily she made her way to the hotel veranda, which ran all around the building, just outside their rooms. She stood a moment and looked out over the water, dotted with fishing-sails or darkened by the shadows of great vessels. Then, as no one seemed to be astir, she determined to run all around the veranda for exercise, going swiftly and lightly on her little feet.

"I wouldn't like to wake any people up," she said to herself.

So began the first long, happy day of her experience in the southland, which was so full of delights, of novelty, of beautiful sights and happy experiences that it would be impossible in these limits to mention them. In fact, the story of Pauline Archer would have to be made very long indeed to detail all that she did and all that occurred to her in the southland. And her pleasure was enhanced by the fact that, almost from the first, her mother began to improve and was able to sit out upon the veranda a great part of every day. Pauline continued her habit of daily talks with her mother, only that these occurred more frequently and with less danger of overtiring the invalid.

"I feel rather as if I had been in a dream," said Pauline, "and might wake any day to find a good many things gone."

"I am so glad you are enjoying it all," said Mrs. Archer.

"And you can enjoy some of it," said Pauline, "you are so much better. You will be quite well by the time we go back to New York, but then I shall be gone away."

For Pauline knew that it had been decided she was to go to school for the winter term. She had an abnormal fear of school, being so shy as to dread being placed among a lot of strange girls.

"Don't let that spoil your present enjoyment," said Mrs. Archer. "You will find as you grow older that things we dread are never so bad as they seem, and everything passes quickly."

"After I go to school," said Pauline, with a quaint little air of solemnity, "I won't be a little girl any more. It'll be just as if I came to an end and turned into a big person."

"What an odd idea!" said Mrs. Archer; but her smile was sad, and Pauline did not guess at the pain with which she acknowledged to herself the truth of the child's remark. "But don't think of such things now. Try to be as happy as possible while you stay here. Papa is going to take you on some excursions very soon."

"That will be lovely," said Pauline, and she made a brave effort to please her mother by trying to dismiss all misgivings for the future. "And I am going this afternoon to the Cedar Walk with Rebecca. Oh, I wish you could go there, mamma. The trees just meet over your head—strange, strange trees, not like those we see at home; and some have flowers on them, and there's a nice smooth path with places to sit down, and green bushes and things where I can hide."

"When I am stronger we shall take some drives," said Mrs. Archer, "and then you can show me everything. But here is Rebecca coming to get you."

"We are going to pick some bananas," said Pauline, "and Rebecca is going to take me another day to get some fruit 'with a queer name,' Rebecca said."

"Pomegranates, perhaps," said her mother. "You will see how very pretty they are."

"I once read a lovely story where there were pomegranates," said Pauline; "they sound rather nice and like fairy-stories."

As Pauline walked away with Rebecca, Reginald Archer strolled over to his wife, seating himself on the rail of the veranda beside her chair. She repeated to him what Pauline had said about coming to an end when she went to school.

"I suppose it's true, in a measure," he said rather ruefully. "She'll boil down to be like all the others. She's a bit different now."

"I fancy she will always have an original mind," said Mrs. Archer, "but I suppose she must lose some of her individuality." Then she added after a pause: "It's hard having to send her away. But I believe it's for the best. She might grow up too self-absorbed and become even morbid."

"She has too much pluck and grit for that," said Reginald. "But if she's so soon to come to an end, we must give her a good send-off while she's here. You don't mind my talking slang, Ada?"

"You're incurable in that line, Reggie," said his wife, with her sweet smile. She was really pleased at his appreciation of the finer points of Pauline's character. Men are sometimes careless in observing such things.

Meanwhile Pauline was at the Cedar Walk, busily engaged with the variety of plays she invented for herself. This new and strange world gave her fancy new scope. The flowers were people, the shrubbery was a forest, and she was alternately a hermit, an outlaw, a hunter, or an animal. Sometimes she was even a bird.

Rebecca sat sunning herself on one of the benches, with that happy faculty for doing nothing which so many people possess. All the time Pauline darted in and out of the thickets, hiding in the tall grass, standing in the midst of flowering shrubs, or swinging herself on the branches of trees. The heat never seemed to affect her any more than did the sun, peeping under her wide hat, impair the exquisite fairness of her skin. Rebecca, on the other hand, declared that the sun and the air made her drowsy and feel "jest like sittin' still." Being engaged, then, in her favorite occupation, and presently nodding asleep, she was startled by a hissing, rustling, and crackling in the grass just behind her.

"Hist!" cried she, starting, "what's that?" Her vague fears in these regions were equally divided between wild beasts and snakes.

"Sakes alive!" she muttered, "I hope it's none of them things."

Her senses being partially dulled by the forty winks she had been taking, she sat perfectly still, not daring to look around. On and on it came, nearer and nearer, still hissing and rustling, till at last the terrified woman felt a clammy substance touch her neck.

"Lord ha' mercy on me!" she cried, springing to her feet. "I'm bit by a serpent!"

"Yes, I'm a serpent, and I just darted out my fang and bit you."

"What's that you say?" cried Rebecca—"'he darted out his fang and bit me'? Then I'm a dead woman."

Pauline was rather puzzled by Rebecca's pantomimic movements and her terrified exclamations. She thought her nurse was entering into the play as she had never taken the trouble to do before.

"I'm a poisonous snake," said Pauline; "my bite is deadly."

"O Lord! O Lord!" groaned Rebecca. "If I had only stayed in New York! I seem to feel the poison going through my veins," added she, turning with abject terror towards the little girl.

"But," said Pauline, stepping forward, with a change of tone, "there is a doctor passing just now."

"Oh, for the land's sake call him!" cried Rebecca, trembling.

"Well, of course. I'm the doctor," said Pauline.

"You?" cried the stupefied Rebecca.

"I'm not the snake any more," said Pauline, "I'm the doctor stepping up to look at your neck and tell you that if he can't find an antidote you'll be dead in a few minutes."

"Great Scott!" cried the nurse. Then, a sudden thought striking her, "Were you only playing?" she asked, with a trembling eagerness which astonished Pauline. She noticed, too, that Rebecca looked very pale.

"Why, of course," said Pauline. In her turn, she began to be a little afraid of Rebecca. "Perhaps she's going crazy," she thought, "from the heat."

"Was it you touched my neck just now?"

"Yes; that was when I was the snake."

"But your hands aren't moist and dank-like," said Rebecca doubtfully, "and I heerd a queer noise."

"That was when I was just darting my fang at you," said Pauline.

"But the cold, clammy thing?" persisted the nurse.

"It was one of those big leaves there," said Pauline.

"The Almighty be praised!" cried Rebecca, casting up her eyes with sanctimonious fervor. Her relief was so great that it was some moments before her wrath began to rise against the innocent cause of her terror.

"The imp of Satan!" she said to herself furiously, "in another minnit I'd ha' swooned away and died, mebbe, of the fright." Aloud she said: "Now I tell you what, Miss Pauline, if ever you dare play a trick like that on me again, I'll tell your pa."

"I didn't mean it for a trick," said Pauline quietly. "I told you I was going to be a snake darting in and out of the grass; but when you fell asleep you must have forgotten."

"I wasn't no more asleep than you were," said Rebecca angrily.

"Weren't you?" queried Pauline. "Oh, well, I just thought you were, because your eyes were closed and your head was down like this."

"Well, anyway, you came near havin' my death at your door, and then you'd be a real murderer," said the nurse viciously.

"Wouldn't it be fearful to be a murderer," said Pauline, half to herself, "and wake in the morning and know that you were! I'm very sorry I frightened you, Rebecca."

Rebecca's face was suddenly wreathed in smiles.

"There's your pa with some gentlemen. I think he wants you, Miss Pauline."

"I hope you're not a snake any more," said one of the gentlemen, as Mr. Archer introduced his little daughter. Pauline, getting very red, wondered how the gentleman knew. As Mr. Archer, too, looked puzzled, the stranger said:

"I witnessed a very amusing little scene just now, where Miss Pauline was not Mother Eve, but the serpent, who very much disturbed the nurse's paradise for a few minutes."

"How was that, Pauline?" asked her father.

"I was a pretending snake, and Rebecca thought I was a real one and got afraid," said Pauline simply.

"No wonder," said her father. "You'd better let her know next time before you undertake so startling a rôle."

He spoke somewhat gravely, but Pauline did not try to excuse herself by saying that her nurse had been asleep.

The strange gentleman who had witnessed the scene took a fancy to Pauline on the spot. From that time forth till the end of their stay he showed her many a kindness. As her father had had a letter of introduction to him, this Mr. Thorpe became a very intimate acquaintance of the Archers, as did his wife and daughter.

Pauline promised Rebecca that she would always let her know when she was about to assume an alarming part.

"When I'm going to be a crocodile snapping about, I'll tell you before."

"I wish you'd snap at something else than me."

"Well, so I can," assented Pauline. "I'll pretend those big white flowers are people's heads."

CHAPTER XIV.

A NEW PLAYMATE.

Mr. Thorpe came to the hotel with his wife and daughter. Mrs. Archer was not well enough to see them, but her husband and Pauline were there. Lucy Thorpe was taller than Pauline and much broader and stouter, with honest brown eyes, and ruddy cheeks that hung down. She was very like her mother, a good-natured and easy-going woman who said very little and that in a deep, almost gruff voice.

Lucy invited Pauline to come over the next day and play tennis with her.

"I don't play very well," said Pauline, "but I like it very much, and if mamma says I may, I'll be sure to go."

"It's good fun," said Lucy.

"I like anything with running in it," said Pauline. "It makes you feel as if you were flying."

"I can't run very fast," said the bigger girl. "I'm rather stout, you see."

"How did you get stout?" inquired Pauline with interest. "I think I'd like to be."

"No, you wouldn't," said Lucy. "But papa and mamma are going now. Be sure you come to-morrow afternoon."

Pauline promised, and the next day, just as the sun was going down a little, Mr. Archer brought Pauline to a long, low house, over the roof of which met flower-laden, sweet-smelling trees. Pauline thought she had never seen so delightful a house, as it stood in that sheltered nook, with deep velvet-like grass all around, interspersed with beds of gorgeous flowers strange to the little girl, and with an orchard in the background full of rich and carefully cultivated tropical fruits. In the garden Pauline first saw a humming-bird, and could scarcely believe at first he was real, his form was so dainty, his brilliant hues shining like gold enamel in the sunlight as he flitted from bough to bough.

She had seen a number of beautiful birds since she came to this region, some of them with many-colored plumage, scarlet or yellow or green, and the sweetest of sweet sounds often reached her ears from the branches of the trees.

"I wouldn't catch him if I could," she said to Lucy Thorpe; "it's nicest to see him on the leaves. He's like a bird out of Grimm's. Perhaps he's an enchanted prince."

Lucy stared.

"What puts all those queer thoughts into your head?" she inquired.

"I don't know," said Pauline reflectively. "Are they queer?"

"Come on, catch the ball!" said Lucy.

Pauline was a perfect treasure for tennis. Her light and graceful form fairly flew over the sward, and as she was always taking exercise in some shape or form, she was what athletes would call in good training. Many an hour was spent in that shaded court in this most fascinating of sports.

Mr. Archer, before they left that first afternoon, invited the Thorpes to join them in the excursion which he meant to take next day in a yacht hired for the purpose.

"I've been to all those places before, of course," said Lucy, "because I was born here, you see; but it will be lots of fun to go there over again with you. And I suppose you'll imagine lots of things."

"Perhaps I may," said Pauline; "I generally do."

"You're an old-fashioned crab," responded Lucy in her hearty way, "but I like you."

Pauline went home to spend a quiet evening hour with her mother, during which they said the Rosary together, as they often did.

"I look forward to these talks," she said gravely.

But indeed she had little idea how the talks with her mother had been instrumental in forming her character. In the first place, they were a safety-valve. Every thought came out freely. Her mother never repressed her, and then there was the opportunity for advice, caution, sympathy.

"You always remember, dear, to say your morning and evening prayers," said her mother on this particular afternoon.

"Oh, yes," said Pauline, "I always remember. I kneel down before Holy Mary's statue and say them very slowly."

"That's right," said Mrs. Archer, "for sometimes, when there are many things to distract us, we forget the one thing necessary."

"I go to church every day for a visit, if I

can," said Pauline. "And then I read one of those little Lives of the Saints you gave me. I always mark the place carefully in the book, and tell Rebecca not to touch it till I come again."

"You learn many wise things that way," said Mrs. Archer, "more than all the learning of the world."

"Are saints always grown up?" asked Pauline.

"No, there have been many children who were saints. They can do God's work just as well."

"*Does* God let children do work for Him?" the little girl asked, looking awe-struck at the sky, which was full of a tropical richness of colors, mellowing, it seemed, the gorgeous hues of the flowers of the luxuriant earth beneath.

"I think He likes their work best of all," said Mrs. Archer.

"I never did any," said Pauline.

"What you have just been telling me— your prayers, your visits to the church, your reading—what is all that but God's work?"

Pauline was still, reflecting.

"Saints always have light at the back of their head, and sometimes they have things in their hands," she observed presently, "and they hold themselves very straight, like this."

Pauline put herself in position, and a ray of the western light fell upon her as an aureola.

"But angels," she continued, "are different. They have wings, and little crowns on their heads, and look this way."

She bent forward, assuming the attitude of the heavenly spirits which she had seen in pictures.

Mrs. Archer always let Pauline talk on as she wished, and more than ever now when the time was drawing near when she would have to find other sympathy and other confidants. She led her on now to speak of her new friend, Lucy Thorpe, and of the projected excursion for the morrow. And then they sat silent a while, the radiance of the sky seeming to melt and blend into the waters till they, too, were as a sea of pearl transfigured. And the glory seemed to enfold the mother and daughter as they sat, apart from all the world for those few moments. It was a type of that spiritual life, the deeper and truer one, which the mother, through the long years of suffering, had planted and fostered in her little daughter.

CHAPTER XV.

A DELIGHTFUL EXCURSION.

The morning dawned bright and fair. Mr. Archer and Pauline were soon joined at the landing by the Thorpes, and it did not take them long to get aboard, that they might enjoy the coolest part of the day.

"We will see as much as we can to-day," observed Mr. Archer. "But I mean to take several days' yachting, till Pauline and I have exhausted the sights."

"That's right," said Mr. Thorpe, "and this is about as good and seaworthy a craft as you could get for the purpose. This man Dick is a good sailor, and his son there is an active lad, who assists him excellently."

The delights of a yachting trip have been often put on paper, but they must be felt to be thoroughly understood. On a fresh, cool day, when the air is brisk and the water a little rough, one sails along before the breeze with the feeling that the world is a new place, with an exhilaration of spirits, a courage, and a cheerfulness scarcely ever to be felt at any other time.

Pauline and Lucy sat together at one end of the boat, their elders at the other. They were both enthusiastic over everything, and communicated their sentiments freely to each other.

"I feel as if I couldn't enjoy myself any more," said Pauline.

It would take far too long to tell all that they saw, as the yacht sailed in and out among those fairy-like islands, with all their wonders, strange to Northern eyes as some Eastern fable. On one of the islands was a huge arsenal and dockyard which Mr. Archer and Mr. Thorpe found very interesting, but for which Pauline did not care very much. They went into an enormous cave, too, hung with stalactites, and the little girl was speechless with awe.

But what Pauline really enjoyed was when she and Lucy were let loose on a coral reef twisted into all sorts of fantastic shapes, and where they heard the history of the busy little insects that work these wonders. There were all sorts of pretty nooks and queer corners about, and caves wherein sea-nymphs or mermaids would have delighted to dwell. They stayed there some time, as it had been agreed that the yachting party should take luncheon ashore. Meantime Pauline played at a variety of games, one of which was that she was a pirate who hospitably entertained a shipwrecked mariner, in the person of Lucy, in her cavern near the sea. The pirate's table was supplied from the contents of a basket which the children carried, every article of food receiving an appropriate name and being brought out, as Pauline said, from "a hole in the rock, which the pirate had for a cupboard."

Pauline had just changed into a mermaid, to the wonder of the prosaic Lucy, and was singing, with a harp made of seaweed stretched upon sticks, when it became time to go aboard the yacht again. They sailed up a beautiful salt lake to explore some places in that direction.

"You must have a look at the Devil's Hole," said Mr. Thorpe. "That isn't a very pretty name for the young ladies, but they may call it 'Neptune's Grotto,' if they like that better."

He showed them, when they had reached the grotto, what a number and variety of fish were darting about in the water, which seemed to catch warm tints from the sun, till it glowed like an opal. As the afternoon was fine and the night promised to be a moonlit one, it was arranged that the yacht should land them for supper at "Fairyland." The name delighted Pauline. How often she and little Mary had talked about an imaginary fairyland! and now she was going to a real one. The fancy could indeed have painted nothing lovelier than this inlet, framed in a wild mass of mangroves, with many-hued aquatic plants, making the shore resplendent with color. Softly above them waved the mysterious calabash-trees sung by the poet. The sky was faintly colored, with streamers of light breaking rainbow-like into pale violet, green, and pink, reflected in the cool crystalline waters, while the moon, dimly visible, arose as though impatient to climb that exquisite horizon. The chime of distant bells seemed the dim echo of some far-away country.

Children are mistakenly supposed to care little for natural scenery, but they very often feel its beauty intensely, without being able to

A Delightful Excursion. 147

express their feelings. It was so with Pauline. The beauty of the scene filled her with a strange happiness. But she said nothing.

As the yacht was about to put out from shore for the homeward journey, the moon sent a soft shower of silver over the water.

"It's made a path for us just big enough to sail upon," said Pauline to Lucy. Her blue eyes fixed themselves upon the orb of night as though she would penetrate the secret which it has kept from the beginning of the world.

"I wonder what it's like up there," she said to Lucy; "if it's a big palace all light, or a city with walls made out of brightness?"

"It's almost as big as our world," said practical Lucy. "I learned that in a book at school."

Pauline continued to look intently upwards for some moments, while the yacht flew on under a favoring breeze, making a line of white foam, silver-tipped by the moon. Mr. Archer and the Thorpes were meantime chatting away pleasantly, while at one end of the boat sat Dick, the master of the craft, and near the little girls was his son, both looking intently and impassively out over the water, as at a mystery they could never solve. Pauline observed the boy near her from time to time, and what was his share in the management of the boat.

"I wish my mother had been with us to-day," said Pauline wistfully; "she would have loved it."

"Your mother's nearly always ill, isn't she?" asked Lucy. "Mine's very strong."

Pauline gave a swift glance at the portly figure and ruddy cheeks of the matron at the other end of the boat, and said:

"Yes, she looks strong, I think."

Mr. Thorpe now called out to her:

"Miss Pauline, I have just been telling your father of some places to which he must take you where you will see very curious things. One of these is monkeyland. We remember *that*, don't we, Lucy?"

"Oh, yes, papa," said Lucy, laughing.

"Well, I want you to give my little favorite an account of our adventures there."

Lucy, nothing loath, began. She was not ordinarily very ready of speech, but this was something so funny, and there was so much to tell, that she did not hesitate.

"You know what monkeys are?" she said to Pauline.

"Oh, yes. I saw some at Central Park, and I liked them; but it would be ever so much nicer to see them in a wood."

"It isn't so nice as you think," said Lucy. "We went into a grove on one of the islands, a good way from here, and at first we didn't see anything, and I was just playing about, when something struck me on the ear. I thought it was papa at first, and jumped up, but he was quite far off. While I was looking, something caught a ribbon I had at my throat and almost choked me, and then began to pull my hair. I screamed and ran away. I stood near a tree, I was so frightened, and just then a hairy paw came round from the other side of the tree and began to claw at my pocket, where there were some nuts. I saw that it was a monkey, and I gave him a slap. He ran up the tree and, sitting on a branch above, jabbered down at me just as if he was scolding or calling me names."

"But you couldn't understand what he said," said Pauline, much interested.

"Of course not," said Lucy, "he wasn't speaking any language."

"Perhaps he spoke a language that other monkeys can understand."

"I don't believe so; it's just jabber, jabber. But I tell you that monkeys are perfect fiends. Another one leaned down from a tree and gave me a horrid pinch. I glared at him, but he was looking another way, as if he hadn't done anything. As soon as I turned my back to call papa, he tickled my neck with the branch of a tree."

"*Did* he?" cried Pauline gleefully.

"Papa thought we'd better run for it, there were such lots of them about; but as soon as we ran, they began to pelt us from above with all kinds of things. A cocoanut almost smashed papa's hat; his head might easily have been broken, and he got hit on the shoulder and had to keep dodging all the time."

Pauline would have liked to laugh, but she wasn't quite sure if it were proper to laugh at a grown-up person's misfortunes. Lucy had no very strong sense of humor and didn't seem to see the comical part of the adventure. Mr. Thorpe, who had been listening, now joined in laughing so heartily himself that Pauline felt free to laugh as much as she pleased.

"I can tell you they peppered us," said Mr. Thorpe, "with nuts, nutshells, and every once in a while with a cocoanut. I tried throwing something back at them, but they replied by a perfect volley, as if they were led on by a trained commander. I struck about with my stick, and that kept them quiet for a minute or two. I suppose they changed their quarters, for they presently bing-banged from another direction, striking my shins and playing the drum on Lucy's hat, their faces grinning at us from every direction, as they hung down from the branches above to have a better shot at us. We made a run for a deserted house that stood just outside the grove, but, bless you! they had a garrison in there, and some big fellows were guarding the door like sentries, and chattering as if they were challenging us.

"These last didn't seem to be very actively hostile," continued Mr. Thorpe. "I gave the fellows at the door some nuts I had with me, and they instantly sat down to crack and eat them. Lucy had some candies which bribed the other belligerents, so that they surrendered at discretion, and we left the whole fortful of them munching away, while we stole out through the door farthest from the grove. So you see, Miss Pauline Archer, what's before you if you go to the country of the monkeys."

It may be supposed that Mrs. Archer got a detailed account of the day's proceedings, and of the funny story that genial Mr. Thorpe had told about the monkeys. Rebecca, who was always curious to hear what was going on, came in for a full share of the narrative. But she got more than she bargained for, Pauline illustrating the subject by suddenly swooping down from a bedpost on the stooping Rebecca, who was engaged in what she called "tidying up" and giving her just "a teenie, weenie pinch."

"You're the plaguiest child!" cried the irate nurse. "I don't think there's a monkey among them could match you for tricks."

"If I could wrinkle my face up," said Pauline, "and if I had long, hairy paws and kid hands."

CHAPTER XVI.

AN ADVENTURE AND A FAREWELL.

OF course it would be hopeless to attempt to tell all that filled up the ensuing weeks of Pauline's stay in the southland. Her mother was so much stronger that they were able to take a number of drives, in all of which they saw so much that was beautiful and instructive that it would fill a volume. It added to Pauline's pleasure to be able to point out to her mother many of the places which were already familiar to herself. But the time for her departure had almost come, and the separation was to be a very trying one for both. Mrs. Archer was obliged to remain in the South the rest of the winter, and Pauline's father was to take their little daughter North to the convent near New York, for the opening of the winter term.

On the day previous to Pauline's departure her father had determined to take her for a farewell sail, and he invited Lucy Thorpe to go with her. It was a lovely afternoon, with every promise of fine weather—a promise which proved all too treacherous. They had been out upon the water for about two hours, when ominous-looking clouds began to come up from the southwest, and Dick, the yachtsman, began to look uneasy and to call out strange orders to the boy which Pauline could not understand. She tried to guess from the boy's face what was meant, but, weather-tanned and impassive, it gave no sign. After a consultation with Mr. Archer, the boat was turned homewards. But it no longer danced gayly over gold-tipped waves, nor did it go so fast, for the wind, though growing every moment stronger, was against them.

The cloud came rolling up over their heads, like a great battleship ploughing the waves. An awful darkness covered the sky. Heavy rain began to fall, lightning to flash, and thunder to growl. Pauline's heart beat quickly, but she gave no sign of fear, while Lucy Thorpe began to cry piteously. No one heeded her, for the energies of the two boatmen and Mr. Archer were taxed to the uttermost. The water lashed furiously about them, the white foam dashing over them, wetting all on board to the skin. The wind howled as it came in fierce blasts against them.

Suddenly an awful thing happened. A wave, a puff of wind, she knew not what, dashed the boy from the place he had occupied, and in a moment Pauline saw his despairing face rising on the waves with an agonized look upon it.

A prayer came swiftly to Pauline's lips: "Sacred Heart, Holy Mary, save him!"

She did not think of herself or of any other for the moment. Lucy Thorpe threw herself down in the bottom of the boat in abject terror, while a cry was heard above the tumult of the storm: the boatman lamenting his son.

"We must put back and try to pick him up," cried Mr. Archer.

"But who'll mind the boat?" cried Dick despairingly. "If you take my place, who'll take his?"

"We must try it," said Mr. Archer, as the boatman only too willingly obeyed him. "At all risks, we must try to save him."

As they drew near the spot, the yacht hurrying now before the wind, the figure of the boy was seen struggling desperately, but with evidently failing strength. The boatman seized a boat-hook.

"God of heaven, if I could let go a moment!" he cried. "But if I do we're all lost."

An inspiration came to Mr. Archer as he glanced at Pauline standing erect and calm, it seemed, as a spirit.

"Can you do this one moment?" he cried, for he had taken the boy's place.

"I'll try," she said, and he put the tiller into her small hands tremblingly, as he rushed to the other end of the vessel to leave Dick free for the attempted rescue. None of them would ever forget that awful moment—the child bending her whole strength to the task, which was no light one for those weak hands in that furious gale. Drenched to the skin, cold, shivering, awe-struck, the brave little heart never quailed. The thought flashed into her mind that perhaps God wanted her to help to save the boy. She had grasped the situation, she knew what was going to be done, and she prayed aloud unconsciously till the boy was thrown into the bottom of the boat, Dick making the first rude attempts at restoration before he abandoned him to fight the battle which was still to be fought before they could reach the shore.

"He will die," he murmured; "but anyway he'll be buried like a Christian in the earth, and that's one consolation."

"Quick," said Mr. Archer, taking Pauline's place, "here's the flask. Pour some into his mouth and rub his hands with it. Then take that rug from under the seat and cover him up."

Pauline was beside the prostrate figure, which under other circumstances would have so terrified her, deftly obeying her father's instructions.

"She's an angel," murmured the boatman to himself, "and no fear about her any more than if she was playing on the beach."

Pauline indeed seemed indifferent to the fearful crashes of thunder, which in her nursery at home, at night-time, used to make her cover her face with the bedclothes. The yacht was rocking furiously, the very toy of the waves, and her light figure rolled from side to side as she knelt at her strange task.

When the storm was over and the yacht lay at anchor at one of the adjoining islands, the boy was carried into a dwelling, where further efforts were made to restore him. But the doctor, hearing what had been done, was of opinion that Pauline had saved his life. The little girl had the joy of seeing her patient open his eyes before she and her father and Lucy Thorpe left the place. Mr. Archer, having arranged that no expense should be spared in caring for the lad, and finding that he was out of danger, hurried home as fast as possible, for he feared the effect of prolonged anxiety on his wife's feeble frame, and he also knew that the Thorpes would be in great distress.

It was only Mrs. Archer's firm faith in God which had sustained her during those terrible hours of suspense.

"I never ceased asking God to take care of you both," said Mrs. Archer.

"And He did in a wonderful manner," said Reginald Archer with unusual solemnity. "If you had been there you would have thought it little short of a miracle. And Pauline is an out-and-out heroine. Only for her pluck we'd all have been drowned."

"You won't tell her so, dearest," requested Mrs. Archer with some anxiety. "Say, if you like, that she did her duty well and bravely, but say no more."

But indeed the heroism of the little girl was on every tongue. Rebecca was constantly finding herself the centre of an enthusiastic group in which the praises of her young charge were sung and in which she joined with gratified pride. The Thorpes, needless to say, fairly wept for joy and gratitude.

Pauline was quite unmoved by all this demonstration; in fact, she did not understand it, nor, even to the day of her death, could she feel that she had done anything extraordinary. The time of her departure was postponed to give her time to recover from the fatigue and excitement and lest any bad effects might follow upon the long exposure to the elements. But her frame, if fragile of mould, was sturdy, and she was soon her own bright self, playing merrily in the sunshine and weaving her pretty fancies.

When at last the dreaded day came, the regret at leaving these lovely scenes and her new friends, the Thorpes, was all swallowed up in the acute sorrow of parting with her mother.

When she went down to get into the carriage with her father and Rebecca, who was to accompany her, quite a crowd had assembled to see her off. Among them were the Thorpes, Lucy and Mrs. Thorpe crying.

"You must come and see us in New York," said Pauline to Lucy, trying to compose her tear-stained face before all these strangers. They promised, mother and daughter, kissing her effusively. Then it was Mr. Thorpe's turn, and the tears were not far from his eyes as he pressed into the child's hand a little parcel. When she opened it afterwards, she found that it was a lovely ring with a miniature upon it set in pearls.

"Remember, you will always have a friend in me," cried the kindly gentleman, "for you saved my Lucy's life, as Dick here tells me. So, good-by and God bless you, Pauline Archer."

His words found an echo and were presently repeated in a hoarse voice close by:

"And so says I from my heart; and over again I says it, God bless you, Pauline Archer."

It was the boatman, Dick, who spoke, the father of the boy who had been saved. Rough as was his appearance and unconventional his words, it was plain that he indeed spoke from the depths of a grateful heart. The crowd, in which was a strong contingent of fisherfolk who had come to have a look at the little heroine, with a few sailors and soldiers from the neighboring fort, took up the cry. For a gallant deed, though it be done by a child, always appeals to the human heart. So the cry was raised and repeated till it rang like a clarion note:

"God bless Pauline Archer! Three cheers for Pauline Archer!"

Pauline shrank back into the carriage "terribly ashamed," as she confided to Rebecca. But her father's face glowed with pride, Rebecca smirked, and the cry went straight to one lonely heart. The mother, a solitary figure, leaned over the railing of the upper balcony, bearing still another of the trials of which her life had been full. It cheered her and gave her hope and confidence, and it brought back to her, by a curious association of ideas, the blessing of the cobbler for her and for Pauline. Surely the benedictions of simple, grateful hearts were a rare treasure for her little daughter to take away with her into that unknown future now beginning. As the carriage drove rapidly away, she saw Pauline leaning out for a last glimpse of her, and caught her farewell wave of the hand. She sank back into her chair, murmuring softly to herself:

"'It seems as if I would come to an end when I go to school and turn into a big person.'"

CHAPTER XVII.

CONCLUSION. PAULINE AT HOME.

It is only necessary to record here that before entering on her new life and becoming a big person Pauline stopped for a day and a night at her home in New York. She found everything the same, only that the house had a queer look of being lonely and neglected, and when the sunshine forced its way into the rooms it seemed to lie there quietly, as it does on Sunday mornings. When she went out upon the steps, there were some of the street-boys, who greeted her with a kind of mocking pleasure, as if she were something that belonged to them. This rather cheered her, though she thought with swelling heart that it would be long before they could call out to her again.

The cook reported that the pigeon was in excellent condition and faithful to his old habit of coming at a certain hour to be fed, though she did not relate that he often had to go away disappointed when she and her niece were taking the air. Pauline waited till it came, and caressed it, and let her tears fall, as of old, while she confided her sorrows to it and bade it farewell, saying solemnly that she would never, never forget it, even when she was big. As she raised her head, she caught sight of the cobbler watching from the foot of the steps, a ray of joy lighting up his worn face like a sunbeam through clouds.

"I'm glad, glad to see you once more, missy," said he, "and many's the day I've walked past the house hoping for a sight of you."

Pauline went down the steps and held out her hand to him.

"I'm very glad to see you, too, and I haven't forgotten little Mary," she said. "I often thought of her while I was away."

"Did you, now?" cried the man with eagerness, as if it gladdened him to know that some one else than himself had given a thought to that vanished presence. "I thought mebbe you'd like to have this," he said, unfastening a little parcel.

Pauline stood by, watching with interest,

her blue eyes fixed upon the package, waiting to see what it contained. It was a rough and highly colored photograph of "little Mary," which he put tremblingly into her hand.

"I got just the two," he said, "there's no one else to care."

Pauline was silent. It gave her a strange feeling to see this representation, rude though it was, of her little playmate.

"I'll keep it always, even when I'm big," she said solemnly.

And the cobbler, being unable to speak from emotion, squeezed the little hand she held out to him hard, and going down the street, vanished out of her life. But Pauline kept her word. She put away that poor photograph among her most precious treasures, keeping it always, in memory of that tiny friend of her youth.

Pauline was soon glad to go in, for the air was sharp and frosty, and she felt the cold more after the genial climate she had been enjoying.

"It's winter now here," she said to Rebecca, "and summer where mamma is. It seems like a dream."

Rebecca was very kind to the child. In her

heart she was fond of her little charge, and sorry at her approaching departure.

"It'll soon be summer now," she said by way of consolation, "and you'll be coming home again for the holidays."

"It will never be the same again," said Pauline, shaking her head.

"You're the most outlandish child," said Rebecca, vexed and depressed by the foreboding. "What difference does a month or two make?"

Pauline did not argue the matter. But she knew, and her eyes looking out of the nursery window seemed trying to penetrate the future which she felt was beginning. Then she asked Rebecca to get her pen and paper and, tired as she was, she wrote a little letter, in a childish, scrawling hand, to her mother, telling her about the journey, about the arrival home, and the simple news of the familiar street. She mentioned Mr. Thorpe's beautiful gift, but, in her loyalty to her little dead friend, she dwelt far more upon the gift which the cobbler had brought her.

Her father came up to the nursery to bid her good-night, and was all kindness and good-nature. Then she lay quietly in her little railed bed, thinking of her mother's solitary figure on the veranda of the hotel which seemed so far away, and of the Thorpes and the cobbler and little Mary. Just as she was falling asleep she thought some one said to her:

"To-night you'll come to an end, to-morrow you'll be some one else." And as a drowsy hum sounded in her ears the voices of the fisher-folk, crying: "God bless Pauline Archer."

www.ingramcontent.com/pod-product-compliance
Lightning Source LLC
Chambersburg PA
CBHW022119160426
43197CB00009B/1081